Praise for
Sober Siblings

"An essential, straightforward, timely and compassionate guide for anyone whose brother or sister suffers from alcoholism."

—MAIA SZALAVITZ, ASSOCIATE PRODUCER, MOYERS ON ADDICTION: CLOSE TO HOME, COAUTHOR OF RECOVERY OPTIONS: THE COMPLETE GUIDE

"Written from love and informed by science, *Sober Siblings* informs and guides readers through the tragedy of addiction. The team of Olsen and Levounis is reminiscent of Bill W. and Dr. Bob, who created a remarkable social network of compassionate help from personal pain and suffering. *Sober Siblings* pays attention to the brothers and sisters in families that have been touched by addiction. This is a beautifully written and organized book. It has a wonderful blend of information, personal stories, straightforward direction, and a good dose of caring. I recommend this book for anyone from any family whose life has been touched by addiction; perhaps more accurately, I recommend this book for everyone. *Sober Siblings* will help those with addiction, those who live with and love them, and the siblings who often get caught in the family crossfire that typically accompanies addiction."

—HOWARD J. SHAFFER, PH.D., C.A.S., ASSOCIATE PROFESSOR, HARVARD MEDICAL SCHOOL; DIRECTOR, DIVISION ON ADDICTIONS, THE CAMBRIDGE HEALTH ALLIANCE

"Pat Olsen's personal story and Petros Levounis' expertise combine for a thoughtful, compelling, and necessary guide. With real-life anecdotes and practical advice, this is a great addition to the field."

"Utilizing both personal and research-based examples, Pat Olsen and Petros Levounis take us into the little explored and often overlooked realm of the 'other' (sober) sibling. Their respectful and realistic approach is candid, humane and practical, covering subjects ranging from choosing the relationship desired with your actively abusing sibling to self empowerment and the choice to disconnect."

Sober Siblings

About the Authors

Patricia Olsen has contributed to numerous columns in the business section of the *New York Times* since 1999. Her features, essays, and profiles have also appeared in the *San Francisco Chronicle* magazine, *USA Weekend, On Wall Street,* the *Chicago Tribune, More* magazine, *Family Circle,* and *Hemispheres,* among other publications. She is a member of the American Medical Writers Association (AMWA), the Association of Health Care Journalists (AHCJ), the American Society of Journalists and Authors (ASJA), and the Society of American Business Editors and Writers (SABEW). She lives in Tinton Falls, New Jersey, and her Web address is www.patolsen.com.

Petros Levounis, MD, MA, is the director of The Addiction Institute of New York and chief of Addiction Psychiatry at St. Luke's and Roosevelt Hospitals in New York City. A graduate of Stanford University and the Psychiatric Institute of Columbia University, Dr. Levounis lectures extensively on addition topics throughout the United States and abroad. He chairs the Committee on Addiction Treatment of the American Psychiatric Association (APA) and cochairs the Public Policy Committee of the American Society of Addiction Medicine (ASAM). In 2008, Dr. Levounis and the Addiction Institute received the coveted Coalition Leadership Award. He lives in New York City, and his Web address is www.AddictionInstituteNY.org

Sober Siblings

How to Help Your Alcoholic Brother
or Sister—and Not Lose Yourself

Patricia Olsen and *Petros Levounis, MD, MA*

Da Capo
LIFE
LONG

A Member of the Perseus Books Group

The American Psychological Association's definition of "substance dependence" appearing in Appendix A, 190–191, is reprinted with permission from the *Diagnostic and Statistical Manual of Mental Disorders*, Fourth Edition, Text Revision (Copyright © 2000). American Psychiatric Association.

Designed by Pauline Brown
Set in 10 point Palatino by the Perseus Books Group

Library of Congress Cataloging-in-Publication Data

Olsen, Patricia.
  Sober siblings : how to help your alcoholic brother or sister and not lose
yourself / Patricia Olsen and Petros Levounis. — 1st Da Capo Press ed.
      p. cm.
  Includes bibliographical references and index.
  ISBN 978-1-60094-055-2 (alk. paper)
  1. Brothers and sisters of alcoholics. 2. Alcoholics—Family relationships.
I. Levounis, Petros. II. Title.
  HV5132.O57 2008
  362.292'3—dc22

                                                                              2008014604

First Da Capo Press edition 2008

Published by Da Capo Press
A Member of the Perseus Books Group
www.dacapopress.com

Da Capo Press books are available at special discounts for bulk purchases in the United States by corporations, institutions, and other organizations. For more information, please contact the Special Markets Department at the Perseus Books Group, 2300 Chestnut Street, Suite 200, Philadelphia, PA 19103, or call (800) 810-4145, extension 5000, or e-mail special.markets @perseusbooks.com.

1 2 3 4 5 6 7 8 9

*To Ann and Katherine, without whom this book
would not have been written*

—Pat Olsen

To my family—Jenny, Panos, George, and Lukas

—Petros Levounis

Contents

Foreword

Alcoholism is an insidious disease: It sneaks up on its victims and their families when we don't expect it. And it is seldom recognized for what it is—a debilitating and damaging illness that destroys a person's relationships, emotional and physical health, and sense of belongingness—until the damage is severe enough that the whole family feels immobilized by it. In the 1980s and 1990s, Anne Smith introduced us to *Grandchildren of Alcoholics;* Robert Ackerman, in his book *Children of Alcoholics,* explained to us the extent of family alcoholism's deleterious impact on early development; and Claudia Black, in *Double Duty,* helped us understand that among children of alcoholics, those with brothers or sisters feel less isolated because they have siblings who share their struggles. Now, a decade or so later, Pat Olsen and Petros Levounis have broadened the discussion with a serious look at the pain, the sadness, and the sense of loss and anger that siblings can experience when a brother or sister becomes an addict.

We know that siblings have a unique relationship that is automatically and positively fostered in a healthy family where honesty and trust and appropriate, loving support are provided throughout a child's critical developmental years. In alcoholic families, however, the relationship—though still unique—is often based on shared survival in a confusing, irrational, and frightening environment. The stories that weave through this compelling book reveal a variety of families and sibling relationships; the common thread is that each sibling has recognized a brother or sister's alcoholism and has taken a particular path to recovery.

When an adult sibling slips into the family disease, feelings of denial and betrayal easily surface, followed by a sense of estrangement and hopelessness that can be devastating. The anger over the loss of a family member who "should have known better" is seen throughout the stories. Many brothers and sisters of alcoholics grow up without the knowledge and skills needed to confront and address alcoholism effectively in an adult sibling.

The authors help us understand that we can hate the disease that has hurt our family and still show love and support for those who are suffering, that it is important to learn about alcoholism and how to address it effectively, and that acknowledging the impact of the disease is the first step to recognizing what is necessary for personal recovery from the pain and losses it causes. Family recovery can be lifelong, and this book provides many suggestions for getting help for your sibling, your family, and yourself. Al-Anon, for example, can help provide the emotional stability needed for that recovery. And family intervention can be the catalyst for change, for recovery of a beloved sibling and his or her own family, and for the healing of the ruptured sibling relationship. There are other options for healing as well. Indeed, these pages offer much in the way of hope and help—for both you and your sibling.

—*Sis Wenger, president and CEO of the National Association
for Children of Alcoholics (NACoA)*

Introduction

To love an alcoholic is to watch in despair as that person sinks to a level he would never willingly choose. Alcoholism robs people of their dreams and their self-respect. It can severely damage their bodies and brains, and left untreated, it can kill. It can also devastate the lives of the people who love them.

Both my brothers are alcoholics. This is the book I wish had existed years ago, for I surely could have used it. My relationship with each of my siblings—or the lack thereof—has informed my life. I've found that others like me have strong feelings about their sibling relationships, too, no matter how long their brothers or sisters have been drinking, or how long since they've stopped. As a journalist who often writes about health, I've written about numerous alcoholics over the years. I told my brothers I wanted to write about our story to help other siblings and they each gave me their blessing.

Picture a cross between actors Jim Carrey and James Woods, and that's what my younger brother Ted looks like. Think of Chuck Norris who's in the Total Gym Fitness infomercial on TV and you've got an idea of my older brother Steve. Or at least that's how they might look if they hadn't abused their bodies. My brothers' years of heavy drinking—and in Ted's case, other drug use—have caught up with them. Neither of them looks very healthy today.

Ted lives in New York State, a few hours from where we grew up in New Jersey, where I still live. Two years ago he spent twelve days in intensive care after taking some street drugs—he's dually addicted. For a time, it was unclear whether he would pull through. Afterward, he was aphasic (unable to speak or understand speech) and the doctors thought he might need long-term care. I visited him on the brain injury ward of the medical center he was sent to, and since then I've talked to him from time to time. He recuperated from the major brain damage, but he still suffers from short-term memory loss. The whole incident threw me for a loop, although I can't say it was unexpected. I'd been dreading something like that for years.

My older brother Steve lives in Georgia. The last time I saw him, three years ago, he was seriously ill with pancreatitis, which is often associated with alcohol abuse. Steve had been sober for more than five years but started drinking again. His relapse, on top of Ted's latest escapade, felt like the second blow of a one-two punch. He's been in and out of the hospital ever since the pancreatitis, blaming his admissions on everything from a bad flu to gastritis—which also can be caused by heavy drinking. Once he said the doctors didn't know what his problem was. He'd simply been avoiding the obvious. When he learned that his latest diagnosis was complications of cirrhosis, Steve could no longer deny the problem. He said that now he'd really have to stop drinking.

Alcoholism has tromped on every aspect of my brothers' lives. Ted has been in rehab seven or eight times. His wife left him several years ago and he has no job and no money. He lives in Section 8 housing and gets food from a food bank. He's been trying to obtain government financial assistance to live on while also scouting for multimillion-dollar commercial properties, presenting them to interested investors, and offering to manage the financial arrangements. Ted has had several businesses over the years, which have probably given him more freedom to indulge in substance abuse than if he tried to hold a job. Now he says he prefers to go after the big money rather than work a menial job just to bring in money. We have a difference of opinion on the wisdom of this.

Steve worked as a telemarketer for the last few years, but when his illnesses kept him out of work he couldn't keep up payments on his car and motorcycle and they were repossessed. He receives social security and a small pension and does little but sit around all day. As with many people who are sick and depressed, his hygiene isn't always what it should be. In one three-month period, he resided in an assisted-living facility, rented a room in a friend's house, and shared his son's apartment. Some months ago I sent him a list of missions offering shelter in his area, should it come to that.

My brothers have few intimate relationships, they seem isolated, and I'm certain these are not the lives they envisioned for themselves. Whenever I think of their unfulfilled potential, their current state, and how it didn't have to be this way, powerful emotions are churned up inside of me. Equally painful has been the disconnected relationship we've had because of their alcohol addiction. Although a friend tells me it's impossible to miss something you never had, I feel the loss of a close relationship with them, and I'm not the only sober sibling who can say that.

There are almost 18 million alcoholics or people who abuse alcohol in the United States—many, if not most, of whom have brothers and sisters.[1] Like alcoholics, we sober siblings are dispersed across all economic classes, age brackets, and walks of life. Even former presidents Jimmy Carter and Bill Clinton know the pain of having an alcoholic sibling (or one who abuses alcohol). No one whose sibling has the disease comes away unscathed, but attention tends to be focused on the alcoholic or on other family members, such as their children or spouses. Yet, whether they like it or not, siblings have a unique bond with each other, and the way in which alcoholism twists that bond deserves special study. To ignore us sober siblings is to omit an important part of the disease's effects.

Your sibling may have just started experiencing problems as a result of his drinking, or he may have been drinking for years. Perhaps he has years of sobriety under his belt, or maybe he's newly sober. He may have relapsed several times. He may even no longer be living, but memories of your relationship linger. Your brother or sister may also be addicted to other substances and suffer from additional mental disorders. There may be other alcoholism in your family as well.

Like me, you may have watched your sibling zigzag from crisis to crisis. At times, you may have been angry, sad, embarrassed, and ashamed about things he's done. You may have beseeched him to stop drinking, avoided him, given him money, answered rambling phone calls late at night, cared for his children, or done any of a number of other things siblings of alcoholics do. Perhaps you've taken part in an intervention in the hope your sibling would enter rehab, or you may consider it in the future.

It is through my own experience, along with stories from other siblings of alcoholics, and aided by the wisdom of an addiction specialist, that I explore the effects of alcoholism on the sibling relationship in the pages that follow. In particular, the book covers the nature and importance of the sibling bond, the experiences and feelings common to sober siblings, and other disorders that may accompany the disease. It also offers effective ways of communicating, surveys the types of support available, provides practical tips, and explores coming to terms with having an alcoholic sibling.

Among the numerous sober siblings I spoke to while writing this book, four share center stage. Rebecca, an aide for the mentally disabled in California who hopes to become a psychologist one day, has a brother who's alcoholic. Kate is a mental health administrator in New York with an alcoholic sister. Bruce, a systems analyst in the Northwest, has two alcoholic brothers. Kristen, an administrative assistant at a Maryland pharmaceutical company who is studying to be a nurse, has a sister who is alcoholic. They, too, want to help others and have offered their experiences and reflections with that hope in mind.

Dr. Petros Levounis, director of The Addiction Institute of New York and chief of Addiction Psychiatry at St. Luke's and Roosevelt Hospitals in New York City, has lent his expertise to this effort, providing extensive insight into siblings' experiences. His direct involvement in addiction treatment programs along with his own private clinical practice have allowed him to examine many family members' addictions firsthand. Indeed, this book is much enhanced by his citations of current medical findings and his helpful observations and analysis.

A wealth of new information about the disease has been uncovered in recent years, and we have provided what we think is cutting-edge information. However, this book is not a substitute for a licensed therapist or the many support facilities available, nor is it meant to be an exhaustive investigation of alcoholism and its effects on sober siblings. It's not meant to criticize your family members, either. But having a brother or sister who's an alcoholic can be difficult at best, and sober siblings are entitled to their feelings. I try to keep one thought foremost in my mind: No one chooses to become an alcoholic. As one young person hooked on alcohol put it: "It's the only disease I get yelled at for having." No one would have blamed him if he got cancer or diabetes. Adult alcoholics suffer from the same discrimination as that teen.

There are those who believe that alcoholics simply have no willpower—that if they had more "character," they would just stop drinking. However, the American Psychiatric Association has classified alcoholism as a disease, which means, in part, that it has identifiable symptoms and follows a progression. And like any other disease, it cannot simply be "willed away." In recent years, research scientists have discovered that alcohol actually changes the brain, which explains why alcoholism is so difficult to treat. The good news, however, is that scientists' greater understanding portends hope for future treatments.

The medical community often uses the terms "alcoholism," "alcohol addiction," and "alcohol dependence" interchangeably.

We use the same convention throughout the book, although in some instances we define these terms further. Note, too, that to be as inclusive as possible we've alternated the use of "he" and "she" between chapters. If you would like some basic information about alcoholism, please see Appendix A. Resources such as the names of books, support groups, and other organizations can be found in Appendix B.

To protect their privacy, siblings' names and identifying details have been changed. Also, my family's history is my version of events, as I recall them. My brothers may remember things differently and may disagree with some of my views.

We hope the sober siblings' stories and comments in this book will make you ponder a number of questions. What type of relationship do you want with your sibling? Are you interacting as effectively as possible, knowing your brother or sister has a disease? How much are you willing to do to help your sibling? How much should you do? What is your responsibility to your brother or sister, if any? Are you focused on your sibling to the detriment of your own life? How can you change that? Finally, what positive traits do you have because you're the sibling of an alcoholic?

We can't guarantee that this book will change your relationship with your brother or sister. In matters of alcohol dependence, there are no easy answers. But our hope is that it will help you gain a greater awareness of your situation, make you realize that you're not alone, and provide examples from which to learn. We also hope this book will help remove some of the stigma that surrounds alcoholism. Finally, it's our wish that *Sober Siblings* will provide support and help you cope as you navigate this difficult path—your journey with your alcohol-dependent sibling.

—Patricia Olsen

—Petros Levounis, MD, MA

1

Uneasy Triad: My Sibling, the Bottle, and Me

*You can't swing a cat and not find someone affected
by drugs and alcohol, whether it's indirectly through
the pocketbook or directly through someone they love.*

—MARTIN SHEEN, ACTOR

Ask people the first word that comes to mind when they hear
the word "sibling" and some will say "rivalry." Others
may answer "bond" or "soulmate." Some siblings are best
friends, while others are distant and have little contact. Same-sex
siblings are usually closest, according to experts, but age differences, geographical distance, and dissimilar temperaments affect the relationship, too. The only given seems to be that the
connection changes during various life stages, as psychothera-
pists Stephen Bank and Michael Kahn note in their seminal book
The Sibling Bond.[1]

No matter what the relationship between brothers and sisters, one fact remains: Siblings have a tie like no other. Even if

we've never been close to our sibling, having the same parents (whether biological or through adoption or marriage) makes the sibling connection—or the lack of it—one of the most significant in our lives. According to writer Anna Quindlen, siblings have possibly the most complex relationship in life,[2] while author Stephen Bank describes the bond as "life's longest relationship, longer . . . for the [sic] most of us . . . than our ties to our parents. It lasts longer than our relationship with our children, certainly longer than with a spouse, and with the exception of a few lucky men and women, longer than with a best friend."[3] We can hold

Nonfiction Books About Siblings

The Sister Knot: Why We Fight, Why We're Jealous, and Why We'll Love Each Other No Matter What by Terry Apter

Brother to a Dragonfly by Will Campbell

Recovering From the Loss of a Sibling by Katherine Fair Donnelly

About My Sisters by Debra Ginsberg

The Sibling Bond by Stephen Bank and Michael Kahn

Special Siblings: Growing Up With Someone With a Disability by Mary McHugh

The Accidental Bond: The Power of Sibling Relationships by Susan Merrell

The History of Swimming by Kim Powers

The Normal One: Life With a Difficult or Damaged Sibling by Jeanne Safer

Riding the Bus With My Sister by Rachel Simon

Three Weeks With My Brother by Micah Sparks and Nicholas Sparks

Brothers and Keepers: A Memoir by John Edgar Wideman

grudges against a sibling, or we can miss them terribly, long after they die.

In *The Normal One: Life with a Difficult or Damaged Sibling,* psychotherapist Jeanne Safer explains that your "siblings are your first peers."[4] In a sense, your brother or sister is "the other you." The two of you (or the three of you, and so on) mirror each other. But for siblings whose brothers or sisters become alcoholics, the mirror is cracked. A sibling's alcoholism twists the bond, with profound effects on the sober brother or sister. We often feel betrayed; disappointed in our siblings; robbed of what might have been a lifelong, intimate relationship; guilty that we escaped the disease; embarrassed by their behavior; and resentful when we're called on to help. I've experienced these emotions and more, and you may have as well.

From Hansel and Gretel to the Waltons to the Hardy Boys, we're inundated in literature and popular culture with images of close sibling bonds. But if a brother or sister falls prey to alcoholism and perhaps abuses other substances or has other disorders (which often accompany the disease), the reality is far different. As Safer says, "A damaged brother or sister will never be a peer, a companion, or a confidant."[5]

For years, whenever anyone asked me how I had escaped the disease when both my brothers (in fact, all my family members) were alcoholic, I was stymied. While I always said I must have taken a hard look at the chaos around me and decided I wasn't going to let the same thing happen to me, that's only part of it.

My brother Ted once told me that I can never understand what addiction has been like for him. That's certainly true. But I doubt he can ever know what his and Steve's addiction has meant to me, either. And I'm not alone. In 2006, HBO, *USA Today*, and Gallup conducted a poll of nearly 1,000 people who were related to someone with a drug or alcohol addiction. Several of the results are telling:

- "Emotional and Devastating/Horrible" were the words most often used to describe the effects of a family member's addiction.

- Almost half of U.S. adults related to someone suffering from the disease of drug or alcohol addiction say they have felt a sense of shame about that family member's addiction.

- Seven out of ten U.S. adults related to someone suffering from the disease of drug or alcohol addiction say that the family member's addiction has had a major or minor effect on their emotional or mental health.

- Nearly 10 percent of those who say a family member's addiction has had a major negative impact on their financial situation say they have had to take out a loan or run up credit-card bills as a direct result of this addiction.

- About a fifth of those who say a family member's addiction has had a major negative impact on their marriage, family relationships, or emotional health say they sought professional counseling.

- While half of U.S. adults with a family member suffering from the disease of drug or alcohol addiction say this addiction has brought their family closer, a third feel it has pushed them apart.

- One third of U.S. adults with a family member suffering from the disease of drug or alcohol addiction say the addiction has caused estrangement among family members.[6]

These results illustrate not only the havoc the disease wreaks but also the fact that family members today are more willing to give voice to their feelings than was the case in the past. In turn, this helps to lessen the stigma surrounding the disease.

Dr. Levounis says:

In some of the sober siblings' stories in this book, either more than one sibling is dependent on alcohol or one or both parents drank. By now the addiction community is convinced that alcohol dependence has a genetic component; if a parent or sibling is alcoholic, then other siblings have a considerably higher chance of becoming alcoholic as well.

My point is not that there's a 100 percent certainty this will happen. Other factors, such as the environment the person is raised in, play a role. However, one of the strongest arguments for the genetic basis of alcoholism has been gleaned from studies on twins who have been adopted by different families and raised apart. In a majority of these cases, researchers found that if a sibling is alcoholic, then an identical twin brother (who has identical genes) has a higher chance of also being alcoholic than a fraternal twin brother (who has somewhat similar but not identical genes), even though they didn't grow up together. Often overlooked, the genetic link is a strong predictor of someone's risk for getting the disease—at times, stronger than the environment in which one is brought up.

Tolerance, or how much a person can drink before feeling its effects, is also influenced by genetics. The genes that code for how much alcohol tolerance a person has seem to parallel the genes that code for the risk of developing the disease of alcoholism. The more drinks it takes a person to get drunk, the higher that person's risk of becoming an alcoholic. It's not necessarily a cause-and-effect relationship, however. Having high tolerance for alcohol is not necessarily the reason someone becomes an alcoholic, and being an alcoholic does not necessarily mean that one has high tolerance. But it seems there is a strong genetic association between being an alcoholic and having high tolerance.

So, if your college-age brother who drinks heavily were to make an appointment with me (or, as is more likely, be mandated to see me by a college counselor as a condition of his probation), he might say, "Doc, I have absolutely nothing to fear—I can have a six-pack and not even feel it. In fact, I can drink everyone under the table at the fraternity house. Therefore, I'll never become an alcoholic like my father or my older brother." He's totally wrong. What he describes actually puts him at the highest risk for alcoholism. He is likely to have a genetic predisposition for alcohol dependence but is being deceived by his ability to drink and not get drunk. He's also in an environment known for binge drinking, which adds a layer of social and environmental risk to his life.

The genetic component of the disease further indicates that alcoholism is not a moral failing. Understanding that your sibling inherited a predisposition to alcohol dependence hopefully can allow for a realistic yet compassionate approach to his illness. Try to keep the genetic aspect of the disease in mind when you're having a difficult time with your family member's drinking.

It's not always easy to remember that alcoholism has a genetic basis when you're fed up with your sibling. Also, educating yourself about the disease does not remove your sibling's responsibility for getting treatment. Just as a person with diabetes or asthma has the responsibility to get help for his illness, so an alcoholic does as well.

Some of us are further along than others in our knowledge of the disease and in accepting that our siblings "got hooked" and absolving them of blame. While there are many voices of siblings throughout this book, below you will meet four whose stories appear most often. As you will see, they exhibit varying connections with their alcoholic brother or sister. You may relate to only some parts of their narratives, or your experience may be totally different from the ones described; but what you will share with all four is having a brother or sister whose life has been ruled by alcohol.

Kristen

Kristen Morgan, 26, a secretary at a Michigan pharmaceutical company, is studying to be a nurse. Kristen grew up surrounded by alcoholism. Her mother has been in recovery for fifteen years but her stepfather, whom she adored, died two years ago of alcohol-related complications. Her half-sister Jenna started drinking and taking drugs when she was 14 and, though just 20 now, has already had several stays in rehab. Jenna got married at 18 but is estranged from her husband and is waitressing and moving from friend's house to friend's house. Kristen doesn't see much of a future for her sister unless Jenna makes a rigorous effort to change.

Her early years with her sister are a blur. The two of them were just trying to survive within a chaotic and sometimes frightening household. Kristen wishes she had more of a relationship with her sister and has reached out to her, but Jenna wants nothing to do with her. "I think she's embarrassed by her life. I've always done better than she has, and I think that makes her feel bad," Kristen said.

Bruce

Bruce Cartwright is a 40-year-old systems analyst in Washington State. He's one of three brothers who were distant even before two of them started drinking heavily in high school. Joe, 45, drank heavily for fifteen years and Nick, 47, has never stopped. Both brothers were "the antithesis of what someone would hope for in a big brother," he wrote in an e-mail, and he still resents them. "They weren't there for me in any of the ways older brothers should be," Bruce added. "They could have done better." Their drinking, when it did start, caused an even greater rift. They crashed several of their cars and were always in trouble, and Bruce quickly tired of their irresponsibility.

Bruce has no desire to patch things up with either of his older brothers and "has accepted the way things are." "You move on," he explained. While some experts report that siblings become closer in adulthood,[7] that doesn't hold true for Bruce and his brothers, or many other siblings of alcoholics.

Rebecca

Rebecca Lewis, 39, of Ohio, was an unexpected addition to the family. Her alcoholic brother Eddie is 55; she also has another brother, Andrew, who is 59. Growing up, Eddie hung around with a group of friends who started drinking in junior high. By his 30s, he was already driving drunk and making a name for himself with the police. Rebecca harangued him for hours. Their father had become an alcoholic in his 50s. How could he let the same thing happen to himself? "I was going to be his savior; I'd make him realize he had to stop," she said. He got worse. Eddie's wife left him and he moved back in with his parents. His father died shortly afterward.

Rebecca spent the next several years trying to protect their mother from her brother's drunken rages. He scared the woman to no end, becoming furious when he wanted a drink and demanding she bring out the liquor she had hidden. Rebecca was married at this point but she lived close by, and she begged her mother to kick Eddie out, to no avail. After some strong words from a judge, he left the state. A few more mishaps landed him in rehab and he finally started putting his life back together in a halfway house. Eddie has had several years in recovery now, and Rebecca says she's discovering a person she never knew.

Kate

Kate Jensen, 52, is big sister to stay-at-home-mom Sarah, 35, who started drinking as a teen. Sarah has two daughters in elementary school who've occasionally found her asleep or drunk at the end of the school day. Kate says Sarah is "just not there for them" as a mother in countless other ways as well. She just can't seem to stay sober.

There's another sister, Melanie, two years younger than Kate, and a brother and sister slightly younger than Sarah. Their parents divorced when the two older sisters were in college, and Kate thinks the divorce contributed heavily to Sarah's drinking. "The three youngest didn't have the same foundation Melanie and I did," Kate said.

Kate has been concerned about Sarah's health and her family for years. A senior administrator in the mental health field, Kate is knowledgeable about the disease and treatment but doesn't feel there's much she can do. And it's not because she lives in New York State, several hours away from Sarah in Pennsylvania. She's tried talking to her sister, but she knows recovery has to come from Sarah. Should she forget, Sarah's husband, a recovering alcoholic himself, reminds her.

The guilt Kate feels about her sister's alcoholism pulls at her heartstrings from time to time. "That could be me," she said. Their mother compounds Kate's self-reproach in that she expects Kate, as both a medical professional and the oldest sibling, to step in and "fix it." Each time Sarah is sober for a while, Kate hopes her sister will stay on the right path.

As these four sober siblings show, alcoholism doesn't discriminate. Research from the National Institute on Alcohol Abuse and Alcoholism (NIAAA) indicates that alcohol abuse and alcoholism cut across gender, race, and nationality. In general, more men than women are alcohol dependent or have alcohol problems, and alcohol dependence is highest among young adults ages 18–29 and lowest among adults ages 65 and older. Also, people who start drinking at an early age—for example, at age

14 or 15 or younger—are at much higher risk of developing alcohol problems at some point in their lives than are people who start drinking at age 21 or after. While there are more male than female alcoholics, and sons of alcoholic fathers seem more predisposed to the disease than daughters, it is also true that women metabolize alcohol differently and become inebriated more quickly than men. In addition, research indicates that a certain amount of alcohol does more damage to a woman's body than to a man's, and in a shorter period of time.

What's the Difference Between Alcohol Dependence and Alcohol Abuse?

According to the NIAAA, alcoholism, or alcohol dependence, is a disease that includes four symptoms:

- *Craving* A strong need, or urge, to drink
- *Loss of control* Not being able to stop drinking once drinking has begun
- *Physical dependence* Withdrawal symptoms, such as nausea, sweating, shakiness, and anxiety after stopping drinking
- *Tolerance* The need to drink increasingly greater amounts of alcohol to get "high"

Alcohol abuse, which can be just as harmful medically, involves similar interpersonal problems—an inability to meet work, school, or family responsibilities; legal problems; drunk-driving arrests; and car crashes.

Dr. Levounis says:

Alcoholism, alcohol dependence, and alcohol addiction all mean the same thing. Unfortunately, however, the unqualified term "dependence" has taken on different meanings in different medical communities, such as internal medicine and addiction psychiatry, and is sometimes confused with the term "physiological dependence." The explanation offered by the American Psychiatric Association, the organization responsible for classifying mental disorders or illnesses, is particularly helpful for family members.

Specifically, according to American Psychiatric Association guidelines, a person does not have to be *physiologically dependent* on alcohol in order to have the illness of alcohol dependence (also called alcohol addiction). Although the majority of people who suffer from alcohol addiction have developed physiological dependence, we talk about having an alcohol addiction only if someone also suffers from significant *psychological and/or social deterioration*—in other words, if the person has intense cravings and has lost control of her life.

The distinction is important. Think of a woman who chronically takes medication for back pain. She will likely become physiologically dependent on the medication (and may experience adverse physiological effects if she stops abruptly), but if she does not exhibit any symptoms of cravings or loss of control, she is probably leading a totally normal daily life. She is not addicted and she does not suffer from the illness of dependence.

Conversely, someone who drinks heavily but is not *physiologically dependent* (does not experience withdrawal) can still screw up her life. Perhaps your sibling has engaged in binge drinking, defined as having five or more drinks on one occasion for a male, and four or more drinks for a female. Binge drinkers can suffer huge psychological and social consequences, and although they're not *physiologically dependent* on alcohol, they can meet criteria for alcohol dependence, according to the American Psychiatric Association.

The significance for sober siblings is that, regardless of whether your brother or sister is physiologically dependent, it's their loss of control that has caused so much pain. Your sibling may abuse other substances or have other mental disorders as well, which can make it doubly hard for her and for you. Hopefully, the information you learn in this book and the resources it provides will help you understand and better cope with this difficult situation.

It's important that everyone addicted to alcohol get the treatment she or he needs, and many choices are available today. Indeed, there is no one treatment that's right for everyone.

Just as the tie to a sibling is for life, alcoholism is a lifelong disease. Some alcoholics stop drinking altogether, and others achieve years of sobriety with occasional relapses. But there is no cure, no magic bullet to ensure that a person will never pick up a drink again—and some people, unfortunately, drink themselves to death. Given that scientists are learning more and more about addiction and the brain, and that researchers are continuing to introduce new drugs, perhaps this won't always be the case. In the meantime, you still need to deal with the daily tribulations of your sibling's illness—which may include dual addictions or other mental disorders.

2

Other Addictions, Other Disorders

Every form of addiction is bad, no matter whether the narcotic be alcohol or morphine or idealism.

—CARL GUSTAV JUNG, SWISS PSYCHIATRIST

Mental illness is nothing to be ashamed of, but stigma and bias shame us all.

—BILL CLINTON, 42ND U.S. PRESIDENT,
RADIO ADDRESS OF JUNE 5, 1999

M*edical experts talk about* the "dually addicted" and the "dually diagnosed" patient. In the medical world, these terms refer to a person who's addicted to another substance besides alcohol (dually addicted) or suffering from an additional mental disorder (dually diagnosed). But for sober siblings, these terms are not just sterile, clinical definitions. They point to the reality that for some of our brothers or sisters—and, indeed, for us—alcohol is not the only challenge.

You may not want to consider that your brother or sister might have additional problems, but because these conditions can further complicate their lives and ours, it's important that we sober siblings know about them. We need to realize that we're not equipped to handle these problems by ourselves any more than we're equipped to handle alcoholism. Perhaps they further signal the possibility that your sibling, and perhaps you, too, could benefit from getting help.

Sober siblings may not think their brother or sister has another disorder. For years, I myself knew only about severe mental disorders such as schizophrenia. Learning about other conditions—and that there were less serious personality disorders—helped explain some things about my brothers. I began to think that some of their behavior wasn't due to their alcoholism alone, and I started reading about other disorders that often co-occur with alcoholism. This is not to say that your sibling has a condition you don't know about. Rather, the point is that most of us probably aren't well-acquainted with the specifics of other disorders; for example, of the four siblings whose stories appear throughout this book, Kate, who works as a professional in the mental health field, is the only one who is knowledgeable about these conditions. If you've long thought your sibling's actions were puzzling (beyond his alcoholic behavior, that is), the present chapter may provide some answers.

Other Addictions: Drugs

Many heavy drinkers are also addicted to nicotine, according to the National Institute on Alcohol Abuse and Alcoholism

(NIAAA). But they can also be dependent on or abuse prescription medications and other illicit drugs like heroin, cocaine, crack, ecstasy, or methamphetamine, for instance. In fact, researchers have long noted the high correlation between alcoholism and other drug use. In 1991, according to the NIAAA, when compared to people not dependent on alcohol, alcoholics were found to be

- thirty-five times more likely to use cocaine.
- seventeen times more likely to use sedatives.
- thirteen times more likely to use opioids (e.g., morphine, heroin, oxycodone, and methadone).
- twelve times more likely to use hallucinogens.
- eleven times more likely to use stimulants.
- six times more likely to use marijuana and related drugs.[1]

Researchers have also found that when people abuse another drug besides alcohol, the latter tends to remain their favorite. In a 2000 study reported by Dr. Levounis and Dr. Richard Rosenthal in the *Clinical Textbook of Addictive Disorders,* respondents who abused alcohol and another drug were asked to rank their drug of choice. In the following ranking of the respondents' primary substance of choice, alcohol topped the list:

- Alcohol 79 percent
- Cocaine 72.7 percent
- Marijuana 48.2 percent
- Stimulants 18.6 percent
- Opiates 16.5 percent

- Sedatives 13.7 percent
- Heroin 9.4 percent
- Hallucinogens 5.0 percent[2]

Both alcohol and illicit drugs act on the same pleasure/reward centers in the brain, and taking another drug while drinking may increase the pleasurable effects. However, using the two together increases their addictive effects and can result in other problems. For instance, more dually addicted people drop out of treatment.[3]

This is not to say we shouldn't have hope for our brothers and sisters, but we do need to be realistic about the insidiousness of substance abuse. The statistics indicate that our siblings are at high risk of abusing another substance as well as alcohol and that alcohol will probably remain their drug of choice.

Another problem is that as new drugs are being developed, substance abusers are finding ways to adapt them for illicit use. For example, besides shooting up cocaine, some substance abusers crush OxyContin pills and inject the powder by syringe. It reaches the system all at once this way, and the person gets intoxicated faster and experiences a more intense high than if he takes the drug in time-release pill form.

Dr. Levounis says:

As someone who doesn't abuse alcohol or other drugs, you may have a difficult time understanding how strong a hold these substances have on your brother or sister. The affair with substances often begins early.

We see definite patterns of substance abuse according to age. Up until age 25, people are usually attracted to more than one drug. The medical community occasionally calls substance abusers in this age group "garbage heads" because of their multiple drug use. As substance abusers age, if they continue this behavior into adulthood, the talk then changes to their "drug of choice." For some people, it's alcohol. They'll say, "Alcohol really speaks to me."

There's something unique about alcohol compared to other drugs. From a self-medicating view, it may affect a person's emotions differently. Patients in my facility's drug program often describe alcohol as their "best friend." They may refer to cocaine as their "mistress" and heroin as their "boss," but they talk of alcohol as a "partner," someone they can rely on when friends and lovers have left them. These patients seem to find solace and warmth in alcohol.

The brothers and sisters of the four sober siblings I talked to in-depth represent a range of abusing substances other than alcohol. Bruce recalls that his brother Joe dabbled in cocaine. Rebecca is certain that her brother Eddie snorted cocaine—she saw a line of white powder on a mirror atop his bedroom dresser. But when she confronted his wife at the time, Eddie's spouse swore that they used it only occasionally. Kate's sister has abused Valium and Xanax along with alcohol, even getting multiple doctors to give her prescriptions so she'd have a steady supply of pills.

Kristen's sister Jenna represents a sibling who has had life-long issues with substance addiction. By age 14, Jenna was on an all-too-identifiable path, staying out all night, skipping school, and drinking and smoking pot. Kristen believes her sister has abused cocaine, and possibly heroin and other drugs as well. Often, when Jenna did finally come home, her pupils were dilated, which usually signifies that a person is either high on cocaine or withdrawing from heroin. The plastic bags of white powder that Kristen and her mother found in Jenna's room were the tip-off that she was using hard drugs, even if they couldn't identify the substance. Kristen tried talking to her sister, but Jenna would have none of it.

Three times their mother got Jenna to enter rehab, but she always relapsed in a matter of days. Because the siblings have been so distant lately, Kristen hears about her sister only from their mother, who says she hasn't changed. "There's nothing more we can do," their mother said. Kristen is pensive, or resigned, or perhaps a little of both. "Maybe some day Jenna will grow up," she said.

I have more graphic memories of a sibling's drug use. Years ago a girlfriend of Ted's called me from his apartment after finding a syringe containing traces of blood. She was beside herself, and maybe she didn't realize how much her news upset me, too. I knew Ted had been addicted to Valium once, and I always suspected he abused other drugs as well. (How is it we siblings sense these things?) I assumed, as a result of what his girlfriend said, that he was shooting up cocaine. I recoiled whenever I heard evidence of his drug use, but I had to listen. I felt I needed to know how bad it was, that not knowing was somehow worse than knowing.

Ten years after the syringe episode, Ted met a gracious and compassionate woman, got married, and enjoyed periods of sobriety over the next decade. But he could never sustain them.

His business also went under, which strained his already shaky marriage even further. I'd phone every few months to say hello because I wanted to stay connected to him, and I desperately wanted to hear he was OK. I was probably as anxious for him as he was for himself. One of my calls was answered by his wife, who said he had started disappearing for a couple of days, and when he did return home he saw people outside their kitchen window where there were none and ranted about a conspiracy against him. Paranoia and hallucinations are often associated with stimulant intoxication (cocaine use, for example), or with severe withdrawal from alcoholism.

Ted always said he had an "addictive personality"; maybe you've also heard this phrase from your sibling. A study reported in the *New York Times* found that people who fall prey to addiction exhibit common psychological traits:

- Impulsive behavior, difficulty in delaying gratification, an antisocial personality, and a disposition toward sensation seeking
- A high value on nonconformity combined with a weak commitment to the goals for achievement valued by the society
- A sense of social alienation and a general tolerance for deviance
- A sense of heightened stress. This may help explain why adolescence and other stressful transition periods are often associated with the most severe drug and alcohol problems[4]

I saw some of those traits in Ted.

Dr. Levounis says:

A variety of terms develop around diseases, and it helps some substance abusers and family members to grab onto these terms. Referring to "addictive personality" as a reason for their multiple substance abuse is one way people may try to explain their addictions. Although many personality traits, such as a high level of novelty seeking, can predispose a person to addiction, many of us in the medical community have put aside the concept of an "addictive personality." The more correct term is "personality disorder," and a large number of alcoholics suffer from antisocial personality disorder or borderline personality disorder. However, quite frequently we also find that when a person stops drinking, many of the symptoms of personality disorders (for example, lying, cheating, and stealing) disappear. In these cases, we don't even consider that the person has a personality disorder; we call these symptoms "behaviors in service of sustaining a dependence."

There are some common traits among people who suffer from addictive disorders, but it's a question of which came first, the chicken or the egg. Did the addict's nonconformity, for instance, fuel his drug addiction, or did his drug addiction lead to his nonconformity? Is he engaging in a certain behavior in order to survive? Addiction is no walk in the park. The addict has to make sure he's using safely and doesn't perish while he's high. He has to get money in order to buy the substance, and he has to try to avoid legal prosecution. Then the process starts all over again. It's understandable that he would exhibit some troublesome behaviors, but it's difficult to distinguish between those that are tied to an underlying personality trait and those that are due to his drug use.

If your brother or sister is using not just alcohol but another drug as well, you may be concerned about how he'll find help for both problems. We used to think that the best course of action was to treat the abuse of the severest drug first. (Alcohol falls roughly in the middle.) For instance, a classic response might be "Let's have him quit heroin now and then we'll work on the alcohol or the smoking." The idea was that if the person continued using one substance, he'd have an easier time quitting both—in due time. We no longer believe that. It may sound counterintuitive, but the current data show that addicts have greater success when they quit several substances simultaneously.

We found this to be the case in our own addiction center with alcoholism and nicotine addiction. In 2004 we received a directive from New York State requiring us to have a smoke-free building. Some addicts chose not to attend our addiction treatment program, but for the smokers who did attend, we provided extensive support and treatment for smoking cessation at the same time that we treated them for their drug addiction. We found they were able to quit both smoking and their addiction to another substance. Our data were not conclusive, but when we presented our findings at a national addiction conference, the experts present agreed that the results were significant. The data suggest that continued nicotine use in a newly sober person increases the risk of relapse and further supports the wisdom of stopping everything at once.

As disturbing as addiction is, the more we sober siblings know, the better prepared we are. Later in this chapter, we'll talk more about how your sibling may begin to get help. But first, here's some additional information about addictive behaviors and other mental disorders.

Other Addictions: Behaviors

Apart from substance abuse, there are prevalent behavioral addictions that an alcoholic can suffer. An expert cites these as the top three:

- Gambling
- Sex
- Internet surfing[5]

Substance abuse is more common than behavioral addictions. So if your brother or sister is addicted to gambling, for instance, alcoholism may be a big issue. However, the reverse tends not to be true. Gamblers have a much greater chance of being alcoholic than alcoholics have of being gamblers. About 85 percent of people will gamble at some time in their lives, and about 1–3 percent will develop an addiction to gambling. Since alcoholism is so much more prevalent than gambling—roughly 10 percent of the population are alcoholics and only 1–3 percent are pathological gamblers—it's easy to understand why someone who is a gambler might suffer from alcoholism.[6]

Lawyer Greg Mahoney is addicted to both alcohol and gambling, says his sister Barbara. He's a Harvard Law School graduate who worked for a law firm in Maine, but he "threw it all away" because of his addictions, she adds. For years Barbara suspected that Greg had a gambling problem because he lived in a tiny apartment and never seemed to have any money. Her suspicions were confirmed when she was cleaning out his apartment while he was in rehab and found a plastic bag full of betting receipts. She believes he's also addicted to sex.

Jay Parker, an addictions counselor at Internet/Computer Addiction Services in Redmond, Washington, treats numerous alcoholics who are dually addicted. Roughly 40 percent of his clients are recovering substance abusers. He has found that Internet addiction and sex addiction often go hand in hand, are representative of an intimacy disorder, and are often accompanied by alcoholism. To him, the character Norm on *Cheers* is a good example for alcoholics of someone with an intimacy disorder. As Parker puts it: "Recall Norm sitting at the end of the bar for hours, always talking about a wife you never saw."

When you realize how isolated alcoholics may become as a result of their disease, it's not surprising that other behavioral problems may arise.

Dr. Levounis says:

As I explained in Chapter 1, the causes of addiction are multifaceted, as are the paths to recovery. For instance, someone may have become an alcoholic because he suffered a traumatic event and then went to Alcoholics Anonymous and recovered. But trauma is not the only reason someone becomes an alcoholic, and there is no one right path to recovery.

If your sibling has a sex addiction, the Internet provides easier access for him. It also increases the difficulty of separating from the addiction because if he has a computer, sex is everywhere. It's comparable to an alcoholic living on a street that has a lot of bars, or to a diabetic working in a candy store. The temptation to indulge may be much greater.

You will constantly hear people in the medical community talk about the need for more research about addiction, but this need is even greater in the context of multiple interacting addictions. When my colleague Dr. Rosenthal and I were asked to write a textbook chapter about multiple substance dependence, we knew that it would be one of the most difficult tasks we ever undertook because there's simply not much research available.

Medical researchers try to simplify matters when they embark on studying a particular condition or illness. It is hard enough to establish the characteristics of alcohol intoxication, withdrawal, abuse, and dependence (along with their respective treatments); imagine trying to study these conditions in people who also use cocaine and heroin. Yet this is what often happens in real life. Unfortunately, we have very little medical evidence to guide us in evaluating and treating patients with multiple substance dependence.

Other Disorders

Besides the possibility that our alcoholic siblings may abuse other substances and activities, experts say there's a good chance they suffer from other mental disorders as well. But we are a nation quick to label people. Slap a label on someone, or toss out a diagnosis, and it allows us to place people in neat little boxes. "Oh, he's ADHD—that explains why he can't sit still," someone might say, or "She's depressed." Terms like these give us a frame of reference for explaining behavior that makes us uncomfortable or is out of the ordinary. One danger, though, is that labels can sound pejorative. "Alcoholic" is a difficult label for some people, so having to contemplate another as well can add to the burden. People do suffer from disorders that interfere with their daily lives, however, and the danger in not naming diseases—even if it means using labels—is that someone with a treatable illness may go undiagnosed and fail to get the help she needs.

According to the Substance Abuse and Mental Health Services Administration (SAMHSA), alcohol problems and mental health problems are often associated with each other:

> *People with mental health problems face an increased risk for alcohol problems and vice versa. Studies show that the overall prevalence of alcohol dependence is almost twice as high among people with mental disorders than in the general population. It is not clear whether mental health problems are a cause or a result of problems with alcohol dependence. People may use alcohol to cope with a variety of mental health problems. On the other hand, alcoholism can cause a number of problems, such as family conflict, job loss, and financial worries that are likely to result in increased levels of anxiety and depression. Some researchers believe there is a common genetic or early family environmental factor that may contribute to both mental health problems and an alcohol problem in some individuals.[7]*

Any of several mental disorders might co-exist with alcoholism. A few, which we explain briefly later in this chapter, are listed on the following page:

- Bipolar disorder (BD)
- Attention deficit hyperactivity disorder (ADHD)
- Borderline personality disorder (BPD)
- Antisocial personality disorder (ASPD)
- Narcissistic personality disorder (NPD)
- Clinical (major) depression
- Anxiety or generalized anxiety disorder (GAD)
- Eating disorders (anorexia nervosa and bulimia nervosa)
- Severe mental illness, such as schizophrenia

In the last few years I've wondered whether Ted has a disorder associated with alcoholism that was never diagnosed. I'm not a clinician, but my brother's behavior when he's intoxicated (or high on drugs, perhaps) seems far beyond other people's acting out. I asked him if he ever discussed the possibility of an additional diagnosis with a therapist he's been seeing, and he said it hadn't occurred to him.

I hesitated in mentioning this possibility, but I hoped my brother realized I was trying to help him. Thankfully, he was open to the idea that he might have another problem in addition to alcoholism, showing me how far our relationship has progressed over the years. We were able to discuss his disease and his behavior honestly, which was a change.

Dr. Levounis says:

Some people think it's not politically correct for a layperson to diagnose someone, but if you see your sibling not eating or sleeping, for instance, there's no harm in noticing that he might be depressed, or saying that you know this behavior can be associated with depression. Making an intelligent, educated assessment in an effort to help your sibling get help is not the same as diagnosing.

Sometimes, people actually find it comforting to hear a diagnosis, because there may be something in their life eating away at them. Your sibling may be asking "*Why* am I like this? What's wrong with me?" Or you may be wondering "*Why* is my sibling like this?" and also be terribly upset.

We're all interested in the challenges we face in life, and we want to know what's behind them. Hearing a diagnosis—even if it is a dual diagnosis—allows the person to say "OK, double trouble. But at least I've started cracking the code. I can give the beast a name." It can be a relief. The person knows he has symptoms of a certain disorder, but also that there is treatment for it, and he can get relief. I'm not opposed to labels. Having a diagnosis is a starting point. Having the correct diagnosis leads to appropriate treatment.

Following is an explanation of several behavioral disorders associated with alcoholism.

Bipolar Disorder (BD)

The National Institute of Mental Health (NIMH) defines bipolar disorder, also known as manic-depressive illness, as "a brain disorder that causes unusual shifts in a person's mood, energy, and ability to function. Unlike the normal ups and downs that everyone goes through, the symptoms of bipolar disorder are severe. They can damage relationships and result in poor job or school performance and even suicide. Bipolar disorder typically develops in late adolescence or early adulthood. However, sometimes the first symptoms appear during childhood, and some people develop them only later in life. BD is often not recognized as an illness—people may suffer for years before it is properly diagnosed and treated. Like diabetes or heart disease, bipolar disorder is a long-term illness that must be carefully managed throughout a person's life."[8]

Two major components of bipolar disorder are manic episodes and depressive episodes.

Symptoms of mania (or a manic episode) include the following:

- Increased energy, activity, and restlessness
- Excessively "high," overly good, euphoric mood
- Extreme irritability
- Racing thoughts and talking very fast, jumping from one idea to another
- Distractibility, inability to concentrate, little sleep needed
- Unrealistic beliefs in one's abilities and powers
- Poor judgment, spending sprees
- A lasting period of behavior that is different from usual
- Increased sexual drive
- Abuse of drugs, particularly cocaine, alcohol, and sleeping medications
- Provocative, intrusive, or aggressive behavior

Symptoms of depression (or a depressive episode) include the following:

- Lasting sad, anxious, or empty mood
- Feelings of hopelessness or pessimism, guilt, worthlessness, or helplessness

- Loss of interest or pleasure in activities once enjoyed, including sex
- Decreased energy, feeling fatigued or "slowed down"
- Difficulty concentrating, remembering, making decisions
- Restlessness or irritability, sleeping too much, or insomnia
- Change in appetite and/or unintended weight loss or gain
- Chronic pain or other persistent bodily symptoms not caused by physical illness or injury
- Thoughts of death or suicide, or suicide attempts[9]

Attention Deficit Hyperactivity Disorder (ADHD)

ADHD interferes with a person's ability to stay on task and to exercise age-appropriate inhibition. There are several types of ADHD: a predominantly inattentive subtype (sometimes called attention deficit disorder [ADD]), a predominantly hyperactive-impulsive subtype, and a combined subtype. Usually diagnosed in childhood, ADHD can continue into the adult years.

Here are the common symptoms of ADHD, according to the National Institute of Neurological Disorders and Stroke:

- Failure to listen to instructions
- An inability to organize oneself and schoolwork
- Fidgeting with hands and feet
- Talking incessantly
- Leaving projects, chores, and homework unfinished
- Having trouble paying attention and responding to details

Paula Jones, a 45-year-old physical therapist in Tennessee, has an alcoholic brother who was diagnosed with ADHD in third grade. Her brother's drinking has had such a catastrophic effect on their nuclear family and on Paula's and her sister's families that she has taken pains to educate herself about alcoholism and co-existing disorders. "Hank was out of control in childhood," Paula said. "I knew something was wrong back then." He was drinking by age 10. She remembers the police finding him passed out drunk, in a neighborhood kids' fort, at that age.

Paula's experience with her brother also illustrates the confusion that can surround alcoholism and co-existing disorders. In his late teens, Hank was diagnosed with seizure disorder (another term for epilepsy). My brother Ted was as well, around the same age. Both Paula and I now believe that our brothers never had epilepsy; instead, they may have been experiencing blackouts from drinking. When our brothers were teens, it was probably not uncommon for doctors to misdiagnose blackouts associated with alcoholism as something other than what they were.

Borderline Personality Disorder (BPD)

BPD is a serious mental illness that affects a person's moods, relationships, and self-image. In general, people with BPD have a problem regulating their emotions, and their unstable behavior often disrupts family and work life and any hope of planning for the future.[10]

According to *The Harvard Guide to Psychiatry*, this disorder has the most varied symptoms; the main one is the fear of being alone.[11] Additional symptoms are

- feelings of loneliness, emptiness, and rage.
- relationships characterized by devaluation, manipulation, dependency, and self-denial.

While a person with depression or bipolar disorder typically endures the same mood for weeks, a person with BPD may experience intense bouts of anger, depression, and anxiety that last only hours, or at most a day. These may be associated with episodes of impulsive aggression and self-injury. BPD can also co-occur with anxiety disorder, depression, and bipolar disorder, and a person suffering from BPD often exhibits other impulsive behaviors as well, such as excessive spending, binge eating, and risky sex.

Antisocial Personality Disorder (ASPD)

ASPD is the mental disorder most frequently associated with alcoholism. The condition is characterized by a pervasive disregard for and violation of other people's rights, and in some people, a susceptibility to aggression. Also, alcoholics with ASPD typically have earlier onset and a more severe form of alcoholism than alcoholics without ASPD. Finally, the incidence of ASPD is higher among prisoners and people in alcohol treatment programs than in the general population.[12]

As Dr. Levounis noted earlier about disorders in general, behavior associated with ASPD could actually be due to alcohol dependence and not the disorder itself. Diagnosis includes behavior starting before the age of 15 and the presence of at least three of the common symptoms. (Although "antisocial personality" is sometimes used interchangeably with the terms "sociopath" and "psychopath," ASPD is not the same as psychopathy or sociopathy. Diagnosis is complicated and must be done by a qualified professional—hopefully someone skilled in dual diagnosis.)

Some common symptoms of ASPD are listed below:

- Repeated criminal acts
- Deceitfulness
- Impulsiveness
- Repeated fights or assaults
- Disregard for the safety of others
- Irresponsibility
- Lack of remorse

Unfortunately, some of our siblings have exhibited this behavior when their alcoholism has progressed. Bar fights, stealing money, taking vacations they can ill afford—some of us know only too well the horrendous acts an alcoholic is capable of, whether he truly has ASPD or not. This is when we may be most angry, and when we most need to step away and try to calm down.

Dr. Levounis says:

To the medical community, patients with borderline personality disorder and those with antisocial personality disorder present (or appear or behave) quite differently. BPD traits drive the people around the patient absolutely crazy. BPD is the classic disorder that causes anger and rage toward the patient from professionals and the patient's loved ones. These emotions are often at the expense of any compassion for the person and negatively affect the care we should be offering the patient. In other words, even doctors have a hard time with patients who have this disorder.

People suffering from ASPD con other people. They're the criminals who lie, steal, and cheat. This makes people angry at them, of course, but not in the same psychological fashion as a person with BPD makes them angry. For instance, borderline patients are often able to project onto you their feelings of being grossly unattractive and despicable. They not only tell you that you are these things but also have the ability to make you identify with these traits and make you feel they're right. That's what hurts so much and stirs up very strong emotions in people's psyches. We call this projective identification.

BPD is a core issue for the person on the receiving end. If someone steals from you, for instance, you're going to be very angry, but not as much as if someone convinces you that you're an ugly person because of their own issues. It's true that ASPD sufferers are the ones who often end up in jail, but they're "cooler," psychologically.

We used to think that only men were antisocial and only women suffered from BPD, but now we know that there are plenty of antisocial women and plenty of borderline men.

For instance, "Mary," a medical student working in the dual-diagnosis unit of a substance abuse center, befriended "Sally," a patient diagnosed with both alcoholism and borderline personality disorder. Mary was conscientious and would stay after her shift to gather additional information about Sally. The next morning she'd come to rounds and share the information she had gathered. Mary was spending considerable time with this patient, and over time Sally gained Mary's trust. But then Sally turned the tables on her. She started by saying "You helped me so much, and you're really a true friend. I want to do the same for you."

"I don't see a ring on your finger so I assume you're not married," she continued. "The reason is, well, because you're so unattractive. I really want to help; you could really use an unbiased viewpoint. You need to lose weight—your belly is so big it's hanging over your pants. And you've got to do something about your hair. It's so stringy and lifeless. You've got a dark moustache that's very obvious, and that ugly mole on your cheek is noticeable, too. You also need a different type of shoe—those make your feet look humongous. Men don't like women with big feet. It's really not too late for braces, either, and you might want to think about whitening your teeth. I'll keep thinking and let you know what else would make you more attractive to men."

The next day the medical student was in tears when she reported to us. Not only did she feel terrible about her appearance, she felt the patient had betrayed her. The truth is that Sally felt despicable and ugly herself, and a way to defend herself against her own feelings was to project them onto someone else. Think of a mentally ill person at a subway station yelling "You're ugly!" at you. There's a critical difference between an incident like this and what happened to Mary. You don't identify with a mentally ill stranger at a subway, so it's a mere annoyance. But Sally went to great lengths to gain Mary's trust, so that Mary identified with her. Mary, the medical student in training, would have been better served if she had received proper supervision to maintain her professional distance, which, in turn, would have protected her from experiencing Sally's rage. Siblings with a similar condition may relate to their sober brothers and sisters in this way.

Narcissistic Personality Disorder (NPD)

NPD begins in early adulthood and is characterized by a pervasive and severe pattern of grandiosity. A world record holder who claims to be "the best" in a sport may be bragging, but she does not have NPD. On the other hand, consider the soldier who claims to have had an illustrious career in battle but in reality held a desk job. That's an example of grandiosity.

According to the *Diagnostic and Statistical Manual of Mental Disorders* (DSM), a person with NPD

- has a heightened sense of self-importance, builds himself up, and wants to be perceived as above everyone else.
- is overly concerned with success, power, looks, or the like.
- has a need to be looked up to.
- has a feeling of entitlement.
- exploits or takes advantage of others.
- lacks sympathy.
- believes others are envious of him or her or is envious of others.
- is arrogant.

Depression or Depressive Disorder

Depression, or a depressive disorder, affects not only a person's mood and thoughts but his or her body as well. And there are several types, from the depressive episodes associated with bipolar disorder to major depression. A person can have just one disabling episode of depression, but usually it occurs several times in a lifetime.

Depression affects a person's sleep, eating habits, self-image, and view of the world. It's not just a bad mood, and telling him to look on the bright side, or to be thankful for all he has, is useless. If left untreated, symptoms can last for weeks, months, or years. The severity and number of symptoms vary from person to person, and may change over time, too.

Here are some symptoms of depression:

- Persistent sad, anxious, or "empty" mood
- Feelings of hopelessness, pessimism, guilt, worthlessness, helplessness
- Loss of interest or pleasure in hobbies and activities, including sex
- Decreased energy, fatigue, feeling "slowed down"
- Difficulty concentrating, remembering, making decisions
- Insomnia, early-morning awakening, or oversleeping
- Appetite and/or weight loss or overeating and weight gain
- Thoughts of death or suicide; suicide attempts
- Restlessness, irritability
- Persistent physical symptoms that do not respond to treatment, such as headaches, digestive disorders, and chronic pain[13]

Depression has hammered my younger brother in the last five years; Ted is one of the 33–67 percent of alcoholics suffering from this malady.[14] "It stops me dead in my tracks," he said. He's finally taking medication under a doctor's watchful eye.

I'd always heard that it's a vicious circle: Alcoholics drink because they're depressed, which makes them more depressed, so they drink more. Or depression makes them drink, which makes them more depressed, which makes them drink more. Alcohol is a depressant to begin with (which means it slows down the central nervous system). In any event, researchers have found that alcoholism and depression are linked.[15] My brother Steve has finally admitted to suffering from depression, too, and says he'll ask a doctor about medication.

The Truth About Suicide

The risk of suicide is high among people suffering from disorders like depression.[16] But experts and researchers continue to explore ways to reach people with mental disorders, and family members can educate themselves about steps to help avert tragedy.

When Ted was in his early 30s and winding down from an especially out-of-control period, I received a disturbing phone call from him. First he said "there were no kicks anymore" and then he mentioned suicide. There went any hope of sleep for me for a few nights, yet I didn't think my brother's call was a cry for help. Instead I felt he was dumping on me, and I resented it. I know now that when someone mentions suicide it should never be taken lightly.

Three other members of my family drank, too. I was unaware of boundaries, so it never occurred to me to try to keep my distance from any of their alcohol-fueled fights or other difficulties. I didn't know what to say to Ted, but I tried to lift his spirits. I talked about being high on life and appreciating everyday things. I think I asked him to get help. I may have called my older brother afterward and pleaded for him to talk to Ted. Steve would only have said, as he always did: "Ted knows what he has to do."

I doubted Ted would take his life, but I spent the next couple of days worrying anyway. Had I known enough, I would at least have given him a suicide hotline number. Often people who are contemplating taking their life just need someone to talk to. On the other hand, depression is serious and the people who man hotlines are trained to try to prevent the possibility.

Arizona resident Samantha Bush, 43, didn't have the chance to talk to her younger brother Tommy when he was feeling hopeless. She was 30 and he was 28 when he took his life. Both had been adopted as babies, and Samantha loved him as if they were biological siblings. "Things started to go wrong when he was in

What Should You Do If Someone Tells You He's Thinking About Suicide?

If someone tells you he is thinking about suicide, you should

- take his distress seriously.
- listen nonjudgmentally.
- help him get to a professional for evaluation and treatment.

People consider suicide when they feel hopeless and unable to see alternative solutions to problems. Suicidal behavior is most often related to a mental disorder (depression) or to alcohol or other substance abuse. It's also more likely to occur when people experience stressful events (major losses, incarceration). If someone is in imminent danger of harming himself or herself, do not leave the person alone. You may need to take emergency steps to get help, such as calling 911. When someone is in a suicidal crisis, it is important to limit access to firearms or other lethal means of committing suicide.

Source: National Institute of Mental Health, "Suicide in the U.S.: Statistics and Prevention." NIH Publication 06–4594 (February 2008). Available online at www.nimh.nih.gov/health/publications/suicide-in-the-us-statistics-and -prevention.shtml.

third grade," she said. The school staff said Tommy had learning problems. Then, when he was moved into a special class, his "more normal friends" dropped him and he started acting out. Samantha knew he had started drinking the day her mother asked her who had been into the cooking wine. She and her brother were still in grammar school.

Tommy kept on drinking and started taking drugs. In his 20s he moved in with his 50-year-old girlfriend. The day the police found her brother lifeless in his car with a self-inflicted shotgun wound was the worst day of her life, Samantha said, and attending his funeral was one of the hardest things she's ever done.

It's hard to find any words of comfort for people like Samantha. When sober siblings feel guilty that they escaped alcoholism, to have that alcoholic brother or sister then take his or her life can seem unbearable. Luckily, we've learned about the danger signs over the years and various organizations disseminate helpful information.

Vicky Crowley, a 36-year-old policewoman in Ohio, is yet another person who knows what it's like to worry about an alcoholic brother's depression. Tim Crowley, 39, has never been able to hold a job for long and has lived with her and other family members on and off. He knows antidepressants can help because he was on them once and it made a world of difference. Vicky even offered to pay for the pills if he'd go to a doctor and start them again, but he always finds an excuse not to go. She thinks it's because one doctor told him he shouldn't drink with the medication. Recently he failed a drug test (he smokes marijuana) for a job that would have paid good money, which exasperated her. Many times she'd like to tell him not to call until he gets treatment. "But I'd feel guilty if I cut him off and anything happened," she said.

For those of us who have been in situations like Vicky's, it can seem like we're between a rock and a hard place—feeling we need to stay in touch with a difficult sibling when we might not really want to. We know we'll feel guilty if our sibling takes his life, so we choose to walk a tightrope. It's tough trying to be there for your brother or sister while at the same time attempting to keep him or her at arm's length. This is an especially difficult situation and really requires that the alcoholic sibling get professional help. The sober sibling can benefit, too, by learning that ultimately we are not responsible for our sibling. Chapters 4 and 5 discuss choosing relationships and establishing boundaries, respectively.

Generalized Anxiety Disorder (GAD)

Almost everyone experiences anxiety at one time or another. But if it lasts six months or longer, says the U.S. Surgeon General, and is accompanied by several other symptoms, then it's more serious.[17] People suffering from GAD tend to worry excessively about work, finances, relationships, family problems, money, potential misfortunes, and deadlines. In addition, they often have trouble sleeping, startle easily, and find it difficult to concentrate.

Here are some physical symptoms of generalized anxiety disorder (GAD):

- Fatigue, headaches
- Muscle tension, muscle aches

- Difficulty swallowing
- Trembling, twitching, irritability
- Sweating, nausea
- Lightheadedness, having to go
  to the bathroom frequently
- Feeling out of breath
- Hot flashes[18]

It seems logical that if an alcoholic is experiencing symptoms like these, he might turn to alcohol for relief. Alcoholism does bring its share of anxiety-producing problems, such as relationship tensions and money difficulties. But, as you can imagine, many of the disorders that accompany our siblings' alcoholism can add to the tensions already present with alcoholism. At times like these, sober siblings should be careful not to become enmeshed in their sibling's life to the detriment of their own well-being.

Dr. Levounis says:

Traditionally, the mental health system and the addiction treatment system have developed along different lines. They have different textbooks, funding, regulatory agencies, and requirements, and many of us believe that the two hardly communicate with each other. Moreover, it is often the case that people who suffer from dually diagnosed conditions and visit a mental health provider are often told to take care of their addiction first, and that people who present to an addiction treatment provider are told to see a psychiatrist first (for their depression, for instance). The systems punt from one to another, and patients fall between the cracks. Communication between the two systems has improved in the last few years, but there is a need for much more work to be done.

We started recognizing this need at our Addiction Institute and established a dual-diagnosis program that begins when a patient enters detoxification. As I noted earlier, there's a tendency toward improved collaboration between mental health and addiction treatment, but in my opinion the two systems continue to be far apart nationwide, and appreciation, identification, and treatment of dual diagnosis are still grossly lacking. In addition, only a limited number of physicians know how to provide treatment. Across the country, only about twenty doctors become board-certified in Addiction Psychiatry every year. There's a dearth of expertise and manpower to fill the need.

When a patient sees a psychiatrist because he's suffering from mental illness, the doctor should ask about alcohol and other drugs of abuse. You may think people will lie in such circumstances, but it's been my experience that the majority don't. They may underestimate their use, but they're usually open and honest. If a person seeks treatment for addiction, the evaluation for mental illness is a little more complicated: Some mental health symptoms are similar to addiction intoxication or withdrawal, and it can be hard to distinguish between them. Occasionally, asking about family history is helpful because both addiction and other mental health disorders have well-established family history components.

A physician can also ask which came first, such as depression or alcoholism, but patients don't always remember; nor do their families. The most helpful indication to determine whether your sibling may have a disorder on top of his addiction is for a professional to learn about the person's periods of sobriety. Alcoholism is a chronic, relapsing illness. Whether he was in jail, in rehab, or attending Alcoholics Anonymous, for instance, an alcoholic usually has a few months or sometimes years of sobriety. We ask the patient, what was your mood like, how was your appetite, how did you sleep, and how was your sex life during those months of sobriety? If we find that most of his symptoms of depression, for instance, persisted throughout the period of sobriety, then we are more confident that the person suffers from an independent depressive disorder and not just from the depressive effects of alcoholism.

In recent years, we have also seen a trend toward overestimating, overdiagnosing, and overtreating disorders. There are patients who seem to suffer from addictive disorders alone who start reformulating their illness in terms of dual diagnosis. They do this for several reasons. First, the popularity of the self-medication hypothesis has prompted people to look for psychological explanations of all their troubles. They say, "I have mood swings, I'm bipolar, so if you give me the right cocktail for my psychiatric disorder, that will stop me from using cocaine." It's a classic way of reformulating a problem in terms of something that may not be there.

Second, today the stigma of depression and mental illness is somewhat less severe than the stigma associated with addiction. There's more work to be done in this area, of course, but several mental illnesses do appear to have become more acceptable. In the past, patients and families would more readily have opted for a diagnosis of addiction. For instance, in the 1960s, they'd often blame experimentation with drugs like LSD in college as the reason they suffered from mental illness later in life. While this may be true in a few cases, it's much less common than people might think. Today, admitting that you suffer from depression, post-traumatic stress disorder (PTSD), ADHD, or bipolar disorder, for example, has less of a stigma than it once did.

Third, from insurance coverage to housing options, medical benefits for mental illness are much higher than those for addiction. The hierarchy is simple: Benefits for physical illnesses are highest, mental illness is next, and addiction is lowest. In addition, the chances of losing your child to the state are much greater if you suffer from an addiction than if you're being treated for a mental illness. If you're caught up in the addiction treatment world, you have a much greater chance of being subjected to regular urine and toxicology examinations—and if the results are positive for cocaine, for instance, you stand a good chance of losing your child. In the mental illness treatment world, by contrast, you're less likely to be subjected to testing so the chances of losing your child are much slimmer.

Also, patients may perceive that the treatment for addictive disorders requires attending long meetings, going to a rehabilitation center, and working hard to achieve and maintain sobriety, while the treatment for depression or anxiety may only entail swallowing a magic pill every morning. The truth is that the optimal treatments for both addiction and other mental illness often require considerable patient effort, above and beyond simply taking a medication.

So, if your alcoholic sibling, who may very well not suffer from any other mental illness, is looking to define himself as primarily having a mental illness, he may find, either consciously or unconsciously, that the mental illness diagnosis is not that onerous. Sometimes, counselors refer their most difficult cases—patients who continue to relapse—to a psychiatrist, insisting that the patients must have a dual diagnosis, when this may or may not be true. The tragedy is that if your alcoholic sibling does suffer from mental illness, there's a good chance he will not be diagnosed or treated adequately—and, conversely, that if he does not, he may end up with medication for mental illness, which he doesn't need. There is danger on both sides—undertreating a true dual diagnosis and overtreating a co-occurring mental disorder that doesn't actually exist. That's why a good assessment is crucial.

Here are some ways your brother or sister might get an assessment of alcoholism or of dual addiction or dual disorder:

- During a visit to a general practitioner or a primary-care clinic

- During a visit to an emergency room
- At an appointment with a mental health clinic or a substance abuse center

- At an appointment with a social worker, a psychologist, or a psychiatrist

- While incarcerated or hospitalized

The treatment of these disorders may involve medication, psychotherapy, individual or group counseling, mutual-help groups such as Alcoholics Anonymous, a residential program, a day or outpatient program, or what's known as SBI, Screening and Brief Intervention, among other options. (SBI involves questioning a patient about his drinking habits and, if the physician believes it's warranted, suggesting that the patient consider taking action.)

We talk about there being "No Wrong Door." The medical community has been working toward having all doctors, and other professionals, screen for alcoholism, dual addictions, and dual disorders. Even prisons are supposed to be helping inmates with these problems. In Chapter 3, on what's up to your brother or sister, and what's up to you, we'll talk about other progress that's being made in this area.

To be co-addicted or have a co-existing disorder is a double burden, and as hard as it may be for sober siblings, one thing we can do is try to be more compassionate. That includes being compassionate toward *ourselves*. It's easy to get caught up in our siblings' dual addictions and co-occurring mental disorders. But knowledge is power, and the more we learn about these conditions, the better able we'll be to deal with our brothers and sisters.

3

What's Up to Your Brother or Sister, and What's Up to You

Our siblings push buttons that cast us in roles we felt sure we had let go of long ago—the baby, the peacekeeper, the caretaker, the avoider. . . . It doesn't seem to matter how much time has elapsed or how far we've traveled. Our brothers and sisters bring us face to face with our former selves and remind us how intricately bound up we are in each other's lives.

—JANE MERSKY LEDER, AUTHOR, IN
BROTHERS & SISTERS: HOW THEY SHAPE OUR LIVES

At the end of an episode of the popular TV program *Grey's Anatomy,* lead character Meredith Grey has this voiceover: "There's an old proverb that says you can't choose your family. You take what the Fates hand you. And like them or not, love them or not, understand them or not . . . you cope."

Meredith could easily be addressing sober siblings. Through no reason other than fate, you're bound to a brother or sister having a horrible disease that affects both their life and yours. As Kristen has said about her alcoholic sister Jenna, sometimes it's inconceivable that anyone who causes themselves and their loved ones so much anguish can continue drinking. You may forget how strong a pull alcohol (and other drugs, if they're co-addicted) can be. But strong it is, and if you're not careful you can be pulled into the maelstrom.

Your Part in Your Sibling's Story

Some sober siblings try to save their brothers and sisters. You get hung up trying to understand them, or you feel guilty, and don't see how your hand-wringing and focusing on their lives is unhelpful to them and harmful to you. Just as your alcoholic sibling can remain trapped in her addiction, you can become stuck obsessing about it or trying to fix it. You need to realize what's her responsibility and what's yours, what you can do and what you can't, and, as the line in the Serenity Prayer puts it, the wisdom to know the difference.

In Chapter 5 we'll discuss boundaries that help in coping, but for now, in this chapter, we'll continue to explore what you're dealing with when it comes to your sibling's addiction. We'll delve more deeply into her thinking and her behavior, the choices she might make, and what all this means to you.

Dr. Levounis says:

Some siblings constantly analyze why their brother or sister became alcoholic. It's their way of trying to cope. If you find you're focusing on your sibling to an inordinate degree, or trying to understand why she became alcoholic, it is natural to feel guilty about it, or even to wonder if you had something to do with it. It's also natural to wonder if your theory agrees with your sibling's theory of her addiction. Whether or not these speculations are true (they typically aren't), they may well have implications for your health, too: If you decide to talk to a professional for yourself, she may ask why you think your sibling became dependent on alcohol. Your answers may help her as she decides how to counsel you.

We find that many people suffering from an addiction have very strong beliefs about why they developed a problem. Alcoholics often say they're addicted because they've been self-medicating to overcome anxiety or depression, or another mental disorder caused by a childhood trauma. This theory even informs the treatment they expect. Their logic seems to be "detox me to get rid of the addiction, medicate me to get rid of the mental disorder I have, and then psychoanalyze me to get to the core of what happened to me. If you're really good at what you do, doctor, then you'll find the root cause of my problem in my childhood, I'll no longer be depressed or anxious, and, as a result, I'll no longer be addicted." We professionals see this as a fantasy that people have regarding their addiction.

It's true that some people do suffer from a childhood trauma and become depressed, for instance, and turn to a drug for comfort. But this is not true in the majority of cases, and, in any case, such an approach does not take genetics or the social and cultural aspects of the environment into account. Plus, you can medicate and psychoanalyze a person all you want, but once the addiction has taken hold, most frequently it requires treatment of its own. Resolving the childhood trauma by itself will not solve all of a person's problems.

Whatever the reason your brother or sister became alcoholic, it's helpful for a counselor to hear about your family dynamics in order to know what direction to take. And there's a good reason to learn your sibling's perception of her disease. The more you know about alcoholism, the better you may understand your sibling's behavior.

A corollary to this is that the better you understand the way an alcoholic thinks, the more you may be able to open the door to treatment, should you so desire.

Once a person suffering from alcoholism agrees to see a professional or seek treatment, a significant part of the work is done. Her denial is starting to erode. The primary-care physician as well as the people at home who are confronted with the alcoholic's denial and would like to see her get help for her addiction carry the big burden of making this "first step on the road to recovery" a reality.

Imagine trying to convince someone that Costa Rica is a nice place to visit if you don't know the first thing about the country. By the same token, if you were to say to your sibling, "I'd really like you to see a doctor," and she says "What's that going to do for me?" it would be helpful if you could answer that question appropriately. You might say, "He's going to talk to you, he's going to evaluate you, and he's going to recommend a course of action." You might add that a doctor could decide that individual counseling is all that's needed, for instance, or that there's medication available that stops the physical cravings associated with alcoholism.

My colleagues and I often encourage family members to gain a basic knowledge of psychotherapy and psychopharmacology. You cannot prescribe medication, but by understanding some of what's involved in addiction treatment, you may be able to assist the experts. Of course we have a bit of concern about this, in case you provide incorrect information. But the important point here is that if you believe your sibling will never agree to see a doctor, then you are disallowing the possibility, whereas if you see yourself as a liaison between her and the medical field, then you leave the door open.

Siblings should not diagnose, however, even if they are physicians. The diagnosis should be done by the professional who takes care of the patient.

By now you should have a good idea of the roles that genetics and environment play in your sibling's disease. But there's another element you have no control over, and that's your sibling's personality, apart from any personality disorder she may have. This is something to keep in mind when trying to cope with your sibling. It's another thing that's "not up to you."

Your Sibling's Environment and Personality

People who don't understand alcoholism may blame or criticize an alcoholic. It's not the alcoholic's fault for getting the disease, but she, too, has a part in her own story that may be quite complex.

Of the four siblings I talked with in-depth, Bruce and Rebecca focused on their siblings' environment as well as their brothers' personalities as possible causes of their addiction. Bruce, the only one of the four with no other alcoholism in the family, attributes his brothers' drinking mainly to their environment. Their small, northwestern town offered few activities for teens twenty years ago, and he theorized that for fun, many of them, including his brothers, turned to drinking. But he adds that there was something that seemed off-balance about Nick, who's still drinking, that set him apart from the other family members. Nick was always nasty and negative, he recalled.

With two alcoholic parents, Rebecca is sure that her brother Eddie was predisposed to the disease. But she, too, places a lot of the blame on his environment and his temperament. In school, her brother was always an outcast, his only friends unpopular boys like himself. He responded by projecting a tough image, and even later, after he had quit school, he still wanted people to think of him as "bad." "It's obvious he had self-esteem issues," Rebecca said.

Along with Bruce and Rebecca, I believe my brothers' personalities contributed to their becoming alcoholics. Ted and Steve were always novelty seekers, which is another element that predisposes some people to alcohol dependence in a family with a history of alcoholism.[1]

Novelty seekers want to "get a buzz on" or participate in an activity that provides an adrenaline rush. This can be anything from constantly looking for a new and exciting vacation destination, to riding roller coasters, to enjoying activities that present above-average speed or risk, such as sky-diving or drag-racing. It's not uncommon for people suffering from alcoholism to engage in such behavior, which has to do with the pleasure/reward centers of the brain.

Some of the behavior associated with novelty seeking is outside society's norms. For instance, many novelty seekers are unfaithful to their partners. Other people may be extremely unhappy in their marriage, but they don't look outside the relationship for solace or excitement. They're not attracted to thrills the way a novelty seeker is. In fact, the majority of committed people, even those who are unhappy, are more attracted to or comfortable with familiarity.[2]

It's not easy to see your sibling taking risks or perhaps being unfaithful to a spouse, especially when there are children involved. Understand that certain personality issues, such as the novelty seeking we've described, may be part of the disease of alcoholism.

Are You Enabling Your Sibling?

Sober siblings find it painful to watch their alcoholic brothers and sisters ruin their lives, so they often end up enabling them, thinking they're helping. "Enabling" is any action that intentionally or unintentionally allows a person to continue her addiction. Examples of enabling behavior include the following:

- Covering up—Providing alibis, making excuses, or taking over someone's responsibilities
- Rationalizing or minimizing the addiction—Developing reasons why the person's continued use is understandable or acceptable, or drinking with her
- Controlling—Trying to take responsibility for the

person's use by throwing out her liquor or drugs or cutting off the supply

- Removing consequences—Bailing the person out of jail or giving her money, for instance[3]

Of course, to stop enabling, sober siblings must be able to step back and recognize what they're doing. You have to realize that it not only doesn't help your brother or sister but actually allows—even helps—him or her to continue drinking. Then you must have the desire to stop what you've been doing. Support groups, which we discuss in Chapter 7, can be helpful for learning more about enabling behavior. Reading about family systems and addiction can also help. You'll find some relevant books listed in Appendix B.

This is not to say it's easy to stop enabling, especially if your sibling is in trouble or ill. When my brother Steve was seriously ill, I felt compelled to send him money for food and prescriptions even though I knew he could also buy alcohol with it. Was I enabling him? Perhaps. But sometimes it's hard to know where to draw the line. No one's perfect, and things are not always black and white. Allow yourself a few gray areas, for your own sanity. Many decisions are hard calls to make, especially when they entail turning your back on a family member.

At the heart of this issue are boundaries, the subject matter of Chapter 5. In short, enabling includes the inability to say no to your sibling as well as the tendency to take up the slack for her or to make excuses for her when it might not be in her best interests to do so. If you don't have good boundaries, it's easy to get caught in the trap of being your sibling's "safety net." Support groups and counselors can help you identify the minefields and change your enabling behavior.

What If There's Additional Alcoholism in the Family?

If there's additional alcoholism or substance abuse in your family, or other mental disorders—for instance, if you grew up in a home with one or two alcoholic parents as Rebecca, Kristen, and I did— you may find it less easy than other people to let your sibling take responsibility for her actions. You may also have a more difficult time coping with her drinking. For instance, you may be overly responsible or overly loyal—or when your sibling has a crisis, it may seem normal. You may not have established healthy boundaries or even know what they are, so you may not understand when you're enabling your sibling.

If there is other alcoholism or substance abuse in your family, your sibling has also been affected by it—not only in the ways that you were but in other ways as well. For instance, some experts believe that due to a lack of parenting, an alcoholic may develop narcissism (self-absorption), though not necessarily severe enough to qualify as narcissistic personality disorder (NPD), explained in Chapter 2. Dr. Edgar Nace, professor of Clinical Psychiatry at the University of Texas Southwestern Medical School, explains how a person might develop narcissistic tendencies and turn to alcohol for solace:

> *The person vulnerable to alcoholism or drug addiction*
> *may enter adult life wounded by . . . failures in being*
> *parented and therefore may retain archaic narcissis-*
> *tic tendencies such as grandiosity (including self-*
> *sufficiency), an overvaluation or devaluation of others,*
> *and a reliance on external supplies and sources to feel*
> *complete. An adult burdened by these narcissistic*
> *themes is doomed to continuous disappointment in*
> *self and others. Depression, anxiety, guilt, and shame*
> *can be expected. It is a short step to the discovery of*
> *relief from such emotional pain through alcohol.*[4]

Note that a person with NPD is self-absorbed to an extreme; she's at the far end of narcissism. But a person with self-esteem is not narcissistic: Feeling confident and capable, standing up for oneself, and feeling worthy as an individual are as it should be. Think of someone you know who's able to laugh at herself; that's a person with healthy self-esteem.

Understanding the effects of other alcoholism in a family can help you understand the interplay among that family's siblings. Consider the support community known as Adult Children of Alcoholics (ACOA), which has developed around the circumstance of having one or more alcoholic parents: Proponents believe that ACOAs exhibit several common traits as a result of the inconsistency and unpredictability of their homelife. For example, since they were unable to control anything about their childhood, they often need to feel they're in control of a situation. They also had to guess at what "normal" is. More detailed information about the effects of growing up with alcoholism, including discussion of the roles that children often assume in an alcoholic family, can be found among the wealth of resources in Appendix B.

Dr. Levounis says:

The psychoanalytic approach, or looking at a person's innermost psyche to explain motives and internal conflicts, is not necessarily wrong, but we put less emphasis on it today than we used to. Indeed, although we recognize that these dynamics may have contributed to alcohol dependence, and that they may sometimes explain part of the patient's behavior, unearthing such early developmental history rarely treats alcoholism successfully.

Consider two siblings of alcoholic parents. Both have received poor parenting. The son becomes alcoholic and develops grandiose ideas, is continually disappointed, and finds relief in alcohol. We say "Aha! Maybe he became an alcoholic and exhibits these tendencies because of his poor parenting." And that's very satisfying until we see that there's a sister who does not exhibit these tendencies and does not become alcoholic. There's a lot of variation as to how each child metabolizes the parental guidance—or lack of it—which, together with the variation as to how the genes shuffle from parent to offspring, results in the luck of the draw to some extent. Alternatively, personality may lead a person to try alcohol for its novelty and become addicted.

Our early childhood experience is influenced not only by genes and parenting but also by peers and, to some degree, by luck. Some people believe that alcoholism is due to unresolved narcissistic tendencies that people carry into adulthood from early childhood experiences. But then we must ask, Is an alcoholic's narcissism, which may involve lying or grandiosity, a core personality trait engraved in early childhood experience, or is it a way to negotiate a life that's out of control? Sometimes it's the former, but often it's the latter. This is another reason you might feel compassion toward your alcoholic brother or sister.

No matter what path leads a person to become an alcoholic, once the disease has taken control we look to the disorder to understand a person's behavior. In other words, often "it's the alcohol talking"; the best way to understand your sibling's behavior is within the context of alcohol dependence.

For instance, a patient I'll call "Laura" told me during an appointment that one advantage of her most recent relapse is that it brought her closer to her mother, who was dying of cancer. She moved back home, as she did whenever she relapsed. Her attitude was: "Isn't it wonderful that this seemingly unfortunate event of my relapse has a positive aspect to it?"

Organizations like Narcotics Anonymous refer to this as "stinking thinking," cognitive distortion that people engage in to accommodate their addiction and try to make sense out of a chaotic and difficult life. We could start analyzing every alcoholic in terms of narcissism or anxiety, for instance, but once again, looking at your sibling's addictive behavior can help you understand that she's caught up in an intricate dance with those around her, as a result of her substance abuse. Chances are that the most straightforward way to understand your sibling is through the lens of someone who suffers from alcohol dependence.

The other aspect of Laura's and perhaps your sibling's disease is the extent to which this is a "family systems" issue. Laura suffers from the addiction, but her family has become enmeshed in it. We further address the subject of giving an alcoholic shelter in Chapter 5, on establishing boundaries.

The Unwilling Caretaker

If you're the person your sibling (or someone on her behalf) always calls for help during a crisis, then you know what a dilemma it can be. You're concerned about her, but, like most people (except perhaps those who have an unhealthy need to be needed or do not understand enabling), you don't want to be put in the role of caretaker.

There are more male than female alcoholics, and traditionally women have been the caregivers and nurturers in our society. But that's not to say it's always sober sisters who are taking care of alcoholic brothers. Families like Penny Howe's have a different dynamic. Brother Kevin, 49, is the one embroiled in their sibling Skip's drinking. In fact, Kevin abets their mother in enabling him.

Skip, 50, has always lived with their 82-year-old mother in the house the siblings grew up in. He has never had a job. "It's a shame," Penny says of her brother. "He's probably the smartest one of all of us, but he's done nothing with his life." She and her four sisters hear about Skip's DUI charges and his bar brawls, but it falls to Kevin, the lawyer in the family, to bail Skip out—sometimes literally. Kevin isn't happy doing this. He does it, Penny explains, for their widowed mother, who can't stand to see Skip suffer any consequences. Whenever Skip gets into trouble, their mother calls Kevin instead of the sisters.

Hearing some families' stories, one gets the impression that a few siblings bear the brunt of caretaking, and that the situation may become extremely complicated when there's an elderly parent involved. A parent's expectations, in turn, can cause additional problems. Recall that Kate's mother, too, wants her to try to "fix" her sister Sarah, both because Kate is the oldest sibling and because she's in the mental health field. And of course Kate hasn't been able to, since she can't control the problem. It's not her problem; it's her sister's.

You may have a certain expertise, such as knowledge of the law, like Kevin, or a background in psychology, or you may have contacts you can call on in these fields. Or, you may be the one who lives closest to your alcoholic sibling. You may help because you don't like to see your brother or sister suffer horrible consequences like losing a job, and as you know from earlier chapters, you may feel guilty that you escaped the disease.

But you don't have to feel responsible, and when stepping in is really enabling, it doesn't help your sibling. It's the alcoholic who has to do the true work, whether that means going to rehab or trying another form of treatment—whatever it takes. Meanwhile, there are things you can do that are not enabling, ranging from talking to your sibling about her drinking to taking part in therapy with her. If you decide to intervene, here are some thoughts.

If You Decide to Talk to Your Sibling

Many of us have talked to our brothers or sisters about their drinking, and more than once in some cases. It's hard not to say something when we're concerned about them, unless we have as distant a relationship as Bruce does with his brothers, for instance. He's the only one of the four siblings highlighted in this book who did not confront his siblings about their addiction.

If you haven't yet had a conversation with your sibling, or if you feel the need to do so again, consider these tips from the Substance Abuse and Mental Health Services Administration (SAMHSA)[5]

- Try to remain calm, unemotional, and factually honest in speaking about your sibling's behavior and its day-to-day consequences.
- Let her know that you are reading and learning about alcohol and other drug abuse, attending Al-Anon, Nar-Anon, Alateen, and other support groups.

Here are some things you should *not* do, according to SAMHSA:

- Don't attempt to punish, threaten, bribe, or preach.
- Don't try to be a martyr. Avoid emotional appeals that may only increase feelings of guilt and the compulsion to drink or use other drugs.
- Don't argue with your sibling when she is impaired or high.

Talking to your sibling may not help, but it may make you feel better to know that you have tried. Your sibling is likely to have a host of defense mechanisms, including externalization (blaming others for her drinking), passivity (a defeated, "what's-the-use?" attitude), and all-or-nothing thinking, according to

Dr. Laurence Westreich, author of *Helping the Addict You Love*. Your alcoholic sister probably isn't even aware of these defense mechanisms, yet your understanding of them will help you know how to respond. Knowing what's behind her statements may also prevent you from getting upset.

Dr. Westreich provides a number of sample conversations that illustrate these mechanisms and how someone might respond. The following—titled "I Just Stopped!"—is an example of what he calls the Flight to Health mechanism, which he describes in terms of an alcoholic saying he doesn't need a support system to stay sober now that he's stopped drinking. I've substituted the word "sibling" for "friend" in the conversation.

> *Sibling:* So, Allan, how's it going with those AA meetings?
>
> *Addict:* I don't know. I haven't gone to any this month.
>
> *Sibling:* I thought you said you were going every day.
>
> *Addict:* Yeah, but I decided I didn't need it. I'm not an addict, really.
>
> *Sibling:* Is that what the therapist said?
>
> *Addict:* Actually, I'm not seeing her anymore either.
>
> *Sibling:* So what are you doing to avoid using anymore?
>
> *Addict:* I just stopped. Isn't that what you wanted?
>
> *Sibling:* Yes, but don't you need some help to stay stopped?
>
> *Addict:* No, I don't. And stop looking at me that way. You told me you wanted me to stop, and I did. So what are you bothering me about?
>
> *Sibling:* I'm worried you'll start using again. I mean, you always have in the past.

Addict: Are you betting against me now?

Sibling: Of course not. I just want you to have the best odds
for staying sober.

Addict: Stop bugging me!

Note that the alcoholic hasn't agreed to seek support, but also that his sibling has successfully voiced her concerns, and calmly. You may find this script and others in the book helpful if and when you choose to talk to your sibling. I approached my brother Steve about a support system recently, and I realize now that I'd have found it helpful to know I could expect a response such as this and to see an example of what to say next and how to stay calm no matter what he said. Of course, real life doesn't follow scripts exactly, but preparation allows us to improvise more intelligently.

If you're unsuccessful in addressing your sibling's defense mechanisms, consider using one of the tactics Dr. Westreich suggests, which is to lay the groundwork for a future conversation. He calls this "setting a trip wire." If your sibling says her drinking is not a problem, ask her what it would look like when someone does have a drinking problem. She might answer "missing work because she's hung over" or "being stopped for a DUI." Then, if she does either of those things, you can remind her that she said this behavior indicates a person has a problem.

Let's say talking to your sibling hasn't worked and you're interested in doing more. For some people, a logical next step may be an intervention.

Tips to Remember When Talking to Your Sibling

- Listen more than you talk.
- Focus on the addictive behaviors you see.
- Avoid lengthy off-the-topic discussions.
- Monitor your own frustration level and stop if you start to feel too frustrated.
- Talk to others who care about the addict. You may learn something useful.
- Be persistent.
- Respect the addict's defenses. He or she has taken a long time to build them up, and it's going to take a long time to bring them down.

Source: Laurence Westreich, MD, *Helping the Addict You Love* (Simon and Schuster, 2007), p. 65.

Interventions

Unless you've been living on Mars, you know that an intervention is a meeting in which family members surprise the alcoholic and confront her in a loving way, with the aid of a professional, in the hope of having her enter a treatment center.

Perhaps you've already taken part in an intervention, or even if you haven't, you may someday. Interventions have helped many alcoholics, but like the theory that an alcoholic has to hit bottom before she can be helped, they've become controversial in the medical community.

Dr. Westreich calls an intervention with a professional a "Formal Intervention" and suggests that loved ones use what he terms "Constructive Coercion" instead. In the latter technique, friends and family talk to the alcoholic individually, over time, employing the same ultimatums as those they would use with professional assistance in a Formal Intervention. (An ultimatum might be "If you don't get help, I'm going to ask you to leave.") The problem with surprising the alcoholic in a Formal Intervention, Dr. Westreich says, is that she's essentially being ambushed, and the tactic often doesn't work. The addict frequently walks out or breaks contact with those who intervene.

If you want to learn more about interventions, we again suggest turning to the resources in Appendix B, or talking to professionals and other people about their experiences. Only you can decide what you're comfortable with and what may be right for you and your sibling.

Dr. Levounis says:

A brother or sister's addiction is very painful to the well sibling, and it's natural to want to help the alcoholic recover. It's understandable that the sober sibling might want to take part in an intervention. Along with other family members, he may see it as a last-ditch effort to try to help his loved one get sober. However, we're finding that an intervention, though a wonderful way to make a family feel they've done something supportive, is typically not all that helpful for the alcoholic.

In addition to what my colleague Dr. Westreich points out, even if an alcoholic does end up packing his suitcase and jetting to a treatment center, he can find himself in trouble when he returns to the environment he left. He faces the same stressors as before, and then the benefits of entering treatment go out the window. The medical community is not as enthusiastic about interventions as it was years ago. The recidivism rate is high, unfortunately.

> On the other hand, there are times when not doing anything can be even more disastrous. The best idea is to give people options. Some treatments may not be as sacred as they once were, but I believe in the "kitchen sink" approach. In other words, give the patient a number of options to find what works best for her. I always make three recommendations to family members dealing with a loved one's addiction: (a) Take care of yourself first, (b) support everything that leads to her recovery, and (c) do not support anything that leads to her drinking.

How Alcoholics Get Treatment

Whether or not your sibling gets treatment is not up to you. What *is* your responsibility is how informed you are or want to be about treatment options. People are often confused about what treatment might actually entail. It doesn't always involve entering a treatment center. Someone who abuses alcohol, such as a binge drinker, may benefit from counseling alone. Support groups like Alcoholics Anonymous are another option. You may also hear that a combination of counseling and medication are a good route. A professional is the one to make recommendations.

If you educate yourself about treatment and recovery, you'll find that many options exist, including an alternative treatment using a plant-based substance. Some options may be dangerous; others are lacking data about their effectiveness. If your sibling does enroll in a program, medical experts agree it should be empirically based; that is, it should be able to provide data illustrating its success rate.

SAMHSA's Center for Substance Abuse Treatment recommends asking the following questions to judge a program:

1. Does the program accept your sibling's insurance? If not, or if your sibling doesn't have insurance, will it work with her on a payment plan or find other means of support for her?

2. Is the program run by state-accredited, licensed, and/or trained professionals?

3. Is the facility clean, organized, and well-run?

4. Does the program encompass the full range of needs of the individual (medical: including infectious diseases; psychological: including co-occurring mental illness; social; vocational; legal; etc.)?

5. Does the treatment program also address sexual orientation and physical disabilities as well as provide age-, gender-, and culture-appropriate treatment services?

6. Is long-term aftercare support and/or guidance encouraged, provided, and maintained?

7. Is there ongoing assessment of an individual's treatment plan to ensure that it meets changing needs?

8. Does the program employ strategies to engage and keep individuals in longer-term treatment, increasing the likelihood of success?

9. Does the program offer counseling (individual or group) and other behavioral therapies to enhance the individual's ability to function in the family/community?

10. Does the program offer medication as part of the treatment regimen, if appropriate?

11. Is there ongoing monitoring of possible relapse to help guide patients back to abstinence?

12. Are services or referrals offered to family members
to ensure that they understand addiction and the
recovery process to help them support the recovering
individual?[6]

Several paths lead an alcoholic to an inpatient program.
Some people may find their own way to a hospital program or
private center. Tyrone Brown, a recovering alcoholic who now
works in a recovery support program in California, has two alcoholic brothers. Some thirty years later, he still recalls the day he
decided to get sober. He walked into his neighborhood bar and
looked around at the regulars perched on a line of bar stools.
They were the same faces he had seen for too long. Then he
thought of the girlfriend who loved him and how he had just
wasted half of a $50,000 settlement from a car accident. "I asked
myself, 'What am I doing?' and I started crying," he said. Tyrone
got up, walked out the door, and entered a sixty-day treatment
program. He keeps hoping his brothers will come to the same re-
alization he did.

A judge may be the one to order your sibling to get treatment,
or, as you saw in a prior section, an intervention with family
members may convince your sibling it's in her best interest to go
to rehab. No matter how an alcoholic finds her way to a treatment
center, the thought of living without alcohol—her crutch—must
be frightening. Some alcoholics also use the excuse that they can't
just up and leave their day-to-day lives.

My brother Ted has referred to his stays in rehab once or twice,
and says he has been in treatment centers seven or eight times.

Whenever I didn't hear from him for long stretches, I figured he was likely either in rehab or in jail. Once he called me from a treatment center and said that his counselor had asked to talk to family members as part of the counseling. But when I called the specialist, the man said he needed my brother's permission to talk to me (this was long before the rigorous patient-privacy policies in place today), and Ted wouldn't give it after all. I wondered if Ted was determined to keep the severity of his problem from the counselor.

It was a bit naïve of me at the time, but I actually thought if I could have told the counselor the true extent of Ted's problems, there was hope for him! I was sure my brother wasn't coming clean about how long he had been drinking and drugging, the jobs he had lost, his money problems, or how violent he could become when he drank. So I'd be his avenging angel, whether he wanted it or not. What I didn't realize was that if Ted was minimizing his substance abuse, he wasn't willing to do the hard work in front of him, and it wasn't up to me to try to force it. My story, like many others, shows that there's nothing you can do when someone simply isn't ready.

Kristen's sister Jenna was in the same rehab facility three times. But if Kristen hoped this would mean a breakthrough with her sister, with heart-to-heart conversations about her sister's addictions, she was sorely disappointed. Jenna mentioned offhandedly that she was enrolling again, but that was the extent of their conversation. She'd never discuss anything about her stay with Kristen afterward, either.

Kate's sister Sarah entered rehab only after a medical crisis. A year after having her first child, she had so much to drink at a party that she passed out shortly afterward. Her husband became concerned and called 911. The medics took her to the hospital, and she ended up in a detox unit. Then Kate was able to convince the staff that her sister needed a rehab program. Sarah stayed sober for a few months afterward, but soon fell into her old pattern.

Maybe you've had a similar experience, one in which you saw a glimmer of hope and thought your sibling was finally on the right path, only to be disappointed. If so, you know how frustrating it can be. Alcoholics have varying degrees of success with rehab, but what's important is that they took that first step to getting well. Since it's a disease of relapse, some people need more than one stay in a treatment center.

If Your Sibling Is Unwilling to Get Help

It's not your responsibility to see that your sibling gets help, nor is it your fault if she doesn't. But understandably, many siblings want to do what they can, so it's important that you be as informed as you need— or want—to be, about the disease and about what might help and what might not.

Even if you've talked to your sibling, if your family has held an intervention, or if she's seen a professional, there's a chance she may be unwilling to do anything about her drinking. If this is the case, here are some tips that may be helpful.

Stop all "cover ups." Family members often make excuses to others or try to protect the alcoholic from the results of his or her drinking. It is important to stop covering for the alcoholic so that she experiences the full consequences of drinking.

Time your conversation. The best time to talk to the drinker is shortly after an alcohol-related problem has occurred—such as a serious family argument or an accident. Choose a time when she is sober, both of you are fairly calm, and you have a chance to talk in private.

Be specific. Tell the family member that you are worried about her drinking. Use examples of the ways in which the drinking has caused problems, including the most recent incident.

State the results. Explain to the drinker what you will do if she doesn't go for help—not to punish her but, rather, to protect yourself from her problems. What you say may range from refusing to go with the person to any social activity where alcohol will be served, to moving out of the house. Don't make any threats you're not prepared to carry out.

Get help. Gather information in advance about treatment options. If the person is willing to get help, call for an appointment with a treatment counselor. Offer to go with the family member on the first visit to a treatment program and/or a support meeting.

Call on a friend. If the family member still refuses to get help, ask a friend to talk with her using the steps just described. A recovering alcoholic may be particularly persuasive, but any person who is caring and nonjudgmental may help. The intervention of more than one person, more than one time, is often necessary to coax an alcoholic to seek help.

Find strength in numbers. With the help of a healthcare professional, some families join with other relatives and friends to confront an alcoholic as a group. This approach should be tried only under the guidance of a professional who is experienced in group intervention. [This is the Formal Intervention described by Dr. Westreich.]

Get support. Remember that you're not alone. Support groups are offered in most communities to help family members understand that they are not responsible for an alcoholic's drinking and that they need to take care of themselves, regardless of whether the alcoholic chooses to get help.

Source: Adapted from NIAAA, "If an Alcoholic Is Unwilling to Get Help, What Can You Do About It?" (February 2007). Available online at www.niaaa.nih.gov/FAQs/General-English/default.htm#help.

Dr. Levounis says:

The ultimate goal is that your sibling gets help, whatever form that takes. But hopefully you realize, after what you've been reading in these pages, that there are different roads to sobriety and not everyone needs the same treatment. The good news is that there's information available on breaking through your sibling's denial, as you saw earlier in the excerpts from Dr. Westreich's book.

No longer does your sibling have to "hit rock bottom" or have a major crisis before she can be reached. For a long time, even in the medical community, we had this idea that alcoholics have to admit their problem and actually want help before we can do anything. We thought the motivation had to come from within rather than from external influences. Medical professionals used to say, "Come to me when you're ready." That's no longer true. We now know how to help people who are not inclined toward treatment.

As first described by Drs. James Prochaska, James Carlo Di-Clemente, and John C. Norcross in 1992, there are five stages of change: precontemplation, contemplation, preparation, action, and maintenance.[7] In the past, we believed a person suffering from alcoholism could be helped only if she had arrived at the *preparation* stage—the point at which she believes she has to change but has not yet taken any steps to do so. The latest thinking, however, is that an alcoholic can be reached much earlier, at the *contemplation* and even the *precontemplation* stage, before she sees the need to change— even if she's in complete denial. Any medical professional can screen for alcoholism when a person simply visits a doctor's office (about a rash or sore throat, for instance). And if the doctor thinks your brother or sister may be drinking to excess, he can suggest getting treatment. Years ago doctors were not trained in such techniques, but as this message has become more widespread in the medical community, it has given us yet another tool with which to fight the disease.

So, there's a better chance today that a family doctor can reach your sibling earlier and can complement the tools you have at your disposal.

Does "Cutting Down" Work?

One of the things you might hear from your sibling is that she'll reduce the amount she drinks, or she won't drink as often, or something similar. Experts call this "moderation management," which is a subset of "harm reduction," and some see it as a viable option in the short term.[8] Harm reduction involves several initiatives regarding substance abuse. One example is passing out needles to addicts in the hope of stopping the spread of HIV and other infections. In one sense, this is reducing possible harm, but in another, it's allowing addicts to continue their substance abuse. Another example is having a designated driver during a night out so that people can drink without worrying about driving under the influence. This removes the danger of having a drunk driver on the road, but if that person is an alcoholic it doesn't address her disease. In effect, it's making the best of a worst-case scenario.

Dr. Levounis says:

Moderation management seems much more helpful for alcohol abuse than for alcohol dependence. Stopping drinking completely—for the rest of one's life—is consistent with the traditions of

Alcoholics Anonymous. It's based on the understanding that once the pleasure/reward pathways of the brain have been hijacked by alcohol, a person is highly vulnerable to relapse for a long time, perhaps the rest of her life. Alcohol dependence (also known as alcoholism) does not lend itself to moderation management because of the person's vulnerability to returning to previous high levels of drinking.

It's a different story with alcohol abuse. Both abstinence models and moderation management models can be helpful in the treatment of alcohol abuse. In short, a doctor can help a person who abuses alcohol reduce and control her use to avoid its most dangerous consequences. This moderation management approach (also called harm reduction, as noted earlier) takes into account the fact that many people may not want or be able to achieve abstinence but can still benefit from counseling and treatment. Recall that if someone is dependent on alcohol, (a) her life is out of control and (b) she most likely has a high tolerance and would experience withdrawal symptoms if she were to stop drinking. By contrast, another person, such as a college student who drinks heavily, may be abusing alcohol but has not necessarily lost control over her life. The latter person is a better candidate for harm reduction.

I treated a college student I'll call "Danny" who got into trouble with alcohol when he was a junior. His grades suffered, and he reached the point where he woke up in a dorm room and had no idea how he got there. In fact, he had suffered a black-out. He was experiencing significant consequences from his drinking and recognized that he had a problem. Danny agreed to stay sober for six months. He was able to pull his life together and graduate with his peers, and he continued seeing me after graduation. He hadn't had a drink since getting sober. Then he asked whether it would ever be safe to drink occasionally in social settings. My recommendation for total abstinence was the safest route, but it was clearly not his intent. The bottom line was that he was able to drink with friends; he didn't resume the heavy drinking he had done in college.

Danny never progressed to the level of alcohol dependence, so, for him, engaging in social drinking after college was not unreasonable. I saw no significant genetic load of alcoholism in his case (in other words, there was no alcoholism in his family), and his abuse had been spurred on by his peer group at the fraternity. Nor did he have any significant co-occurring psychological illness such as depression, anxiety, or attention deficit hyperactivity disorder (ADHD). Danny's case is one in which social drinking turned out to be a safe outcome option.

Regardless of their stance in the abstinence versus harm reduction debate, members of the medical community largely agree that the more severe the alcohol dependence, the more sense abstinence-based treatment models make.

It's natural to have hope for your brother or sister, but don't be disappointed if she stops drinking and then starts again. Relapse is not a sign of failure or weakness; it's part of the disease, and often more than one stay in rehab is necessary if the person is to be successful. A person who is dependent on alcohol can be sober for three years or thirty and still pick up a drink. However, though many people do not stop drinking, the NIAAA offers this hope: "The substantial improvement in patients who do not attain complete abstinence or problem-free reduced drinking is often overlooked."[9]

If your sibling is still in denial, or if you've been contending with years of her alcoholism, Chapter 4, on choosing what type of relationship you want, and Chapter 5, on establishing boundaries, will provide some help.

4

Choosing What Kind of Relationship You Want

One realizes that human relationships . . . can never be wholly satisfactory, that every ego is half the time greedily seeking them, and half the time pulling away from them. In these simple relationships, there are innumerable shades of sweetness and anguish which make up the pattern of our lives day by day.

—WILLA CATHER, U.S. NOVELIST, IN
"KATHERINE MANSFIELD," AN ESSAY IN *WILLA CATHER ON
WRITING: CRITICAL STUDIES ON WRITING AS AN ART*

All relationships ebb and flow. Even so, interacting with an alcoholic sibling can be a far cry from the image of a gentle tide rolling in and out. When a brother or sister is drinking or in the middle of a crisis, it's more like being caught in a Category 5 hurricane. And I doubt any sober sibling can remain totally detached.

If your feelings fluctuate like mine do, depending on how your sibling's doing, and if, because of this ambivalence, you've gone back and forth about how you want to interact with him, this chapter can help—specifically, by offering a few ideas for deciding what kind of relationship you really want. During my brothers' sober periods, we maintained a fairly normal relationship even after our parents died. We were all busy with work and family, but we made it a point to get together regularly. My husband and I used to have dinner with Steve and his wife, for example, and we'd visit Ted's family on the way home from vacation. Our families got together for Christmas, and we marked each others' birthdays with phone calls and cards.

That's all changed now, and it's not just because we don't live near each other. I thought the worst had ended years ago. It hadn't. Ever since Ted's potentially lethal overdose and Steve's string of alcohol-related hospitalizations, I've been struggling with what relationship works best for me with each of them. Sometimes I have a hard time even knowing what to say to my brothers.

Sober siblings are a testament to the fact that alcoholism is a family disease. Besides what your brother's or sister's drinking does to the sibling bond, it affects relationships among nonalcoholics in the family as well.

You and Your Sibling Are Not the Only Ones Involved

From the amount of contact you desire with your sibling to the level of communication that might work best for you, you have choices. The decisions you make are important not only for you but for those you're close to, whether that includes your parents, your spouse, your partner, your significant other, or your children. Your relationship with your sibling affects still others in your circle, too. The effects can reach into your workplace, your social life, and everywhere you might not expect it.

My husband Carl is probably like many loved ones—he's been right there with me in the middle of my brothers' disease. He was there the time I collected Steve from the police station after he was stopped for drunk driving (he drove Steve's car home for him), and he overheard me on countless calls with Steve's daughter and son trying to arrange care for their father after his hospitalizations. Carl also rode with me to the rehabilitation hospital where Ted ended up after his drug overdose. Had my husband not been the person he is, I wouldn't have had nearly as much support. Still, I wonder if he had any idea of what he had signed on for when he married me.

My teenage son is an example of how children of sober siblings also become involved. Ever since I started talking to him about the dangers of alcohol years ago, I've pointed to my brothers as examples. He knows my brother Ted can't be counted on to attend family functions, and once he said he'd had all the bad news he could handle about my brother for a while. At least he never saw Ted drunk. Recall Paula Jones's story in Chapter 2: As it turns out, her children were frightened by her alcoholic brother's behavior on holidays, and she decided to exclude him from future celebrations if he didn't stop drinking. And it's not only children who are affected. Besides nieces and nephews, there are countless aunts and uncles who watch their siblings' children become a part of their parents' illness. Grandparents and members of stepfamilies are still others who are affected.

If your brother or sister has been involved in an alcohol-fueled crisis, then surely someone close to you has felt the aftershock. Rebecca's husband Jerry is another example of the impact on a sober sibling's family member. Recall that when Eddie moved back in with his mother, Rebecca felt she had to protect her widowed mother from her alcoholic brother's rampages. A few days before his sister's wedding, Eddie had a few too many drinks and started heading toward his car. When Rebecca grabbed his car keys, he chased her around the house and attempted to wrestle them back, leaving ugly black-and-blue marks. As a result, Rebecca walked down the aisle with big bruises on her arms. Not only was she not exactly the vision of loveliness her husband Jerry had anticipated, he was dreading the questions from the wedding guests as much as she was.

Eddie also intruded on the newly married couple's Christmas dinner. Rebecca and her husband were celebrating at Jerry's family home when she decided to call her mother. Eddie had gone berserk again and was slamming doors and "yelling his head off," her mother said; but when Rebecca wanted to call the police, her mother was adamant that she do nothing. She just wanted her daughter to stay on the line until Eddie calmed down. Rebecca spent much of the dinner hour on the phone in the den, mad at her brother and feeling guilty that she wasn't with her mother.

If you've confided in friends about your brother or sister, then you can understand how a sibling's behavior can impinge on friendships, too. If my friends charged for all the hours I've leaned on their shoulders about my brothers, I could never pay them in full. Good friends are there in tough times for you, but a wise person knows there's a limit. (If you find you can't stop obsessing about your sibling, this should be a clue that you can't handle the disease alone.)

And if you've ever gotten a phone call at work from your sibling (or about your sibling) you've seen firsthand how a brother's and sister's disease can intrude on your worklife. When I worked at a staid telecommunications firm, Ted tried to call me collect to ask for money. His call went to a receptionist, who visited my desk to inform me, in an arch voice, that collect calls were not allowed. I only hoped my boss didn't get wind of what happened.

Frequently, sober siblings mention their alcoholic brother or sister on an Internet forum. One such posting, on a Web site for police officers, was by a man who seemed worried that his alcoholic brother might hurt his chances for promotion or transfer. He wanted an opinion on whether he should note on an application that his sibling suffers from alcoholism. He was concerned because his brother had been cited for DUI, hadn't attended court-mandated treatment, and had warrants out for his arrest. An officer who responded advised against revealing this information; he reasoned that if he were on the hiring board, he'd worry about what the sober sibling would do should he respond to a call and learn that his brother was the cause of the trouble.

The policeman who posted the question said he has little contact with his brother, by his own choice. But if you want a relationship with your sibling, deciding the best way to interact can help your relationship with him and go a long way toward protecting your sanity.

The above examples show how far alcoholism can affect (and often disrupt) our lives and those of our loved ones—you surely have your own stories. Yet we have a tie with our brothers and sisters, no matter how mad we get, and many of us don't want to break that tie or give up on them totally. That means we have to find a way to communicate with our siblings despite their disease. This is not to say that you should stay in an untenable relationship, or that you should feel guilty if you have walked away or decide to do so in the future. (Later in the chapter we'll discuss cutting ties.)

Dr. Levounis says:

You've seen how an elderly widow might rely on a sober son or daughter for protection from an alcoholic child, or how she may draw one of the children in so that they're actually helping to enable the alcoholic. This is one way in which alcoholic brothers and sisters affect parents. But parents are also affected by the interactions between their sober child and his alcoholic brother or sister.

Often, in well-meaning families, it's reasonable and appropriate for parents to try to love all their children equally. But when alcoholic siblings become toxic to the other children because of their disease, the parents may feel compelled to step in and take sides—an action that creates huge difficulties no matter how well-intentioned. The tension in the sibling relationship translates into strain between the parents, which in turn stresses the relationship between parents and children. Soon everyone in the family is alienated.

An example is a family from my private practice with two children who are college students, "Brad" and "Max." The parents had given each brother a credit card with a limit. Brad, the brother suffering from alcoholism, started abusing the card, so the parents had to rescind it. That made Max feel guilty, so he started financing Brad behind his parents' back. They found out and got upset with Max, and before they knew it the whole family was caught in a vortex of lies, guilt, and resentment. This again illustrates that the relationship between an alcoholic sibling and the sober sibling touches others. The parents had enjoyed a healthy relationship with Max until the credit-card incident, but his attempt to support his brother strained his relationship with his parents.

More than half of all spousal and child abuse has been linked to alcohol abuse, and alcoholics have a divorce rate seven times the national divorce rate. When a family member gets sick, there are practical issues to contend with—but with alcoholism, a layer of anguish is added. Alcoholics have a tremendous amount of self-blame, and as we often see, the burden is so horrific that it comes out as denial. It's much easier for the alcoholic to say he doesn't have a problem than to admit how much he is hurting his family.

The family dynamics become a two-way street. On one hand, the alcoholic may be in denial, but on the other, family members may bring in their own prejudice—they may be particularly aggressive or relentless in their conviction that the alcoholic is simply weak. As we said earlier, family members often think, "If only he had some spine, he'd quit drinking—end of story." After all, a diabetic strains family relationships, too—but no one would ever says something comparable; no one would tell Grandma, who has a compromised pancreas, for instance, to "just stop" being ill. There's something family members find particularly grinding about the alcoholic. No one close to an alcoholic remains unscathed, and the bad feelings that are often directed toward this person can easily spread throughout the family to members of the extended family.

Our Choices—From Ritual Communication to Intimacy

Some time ago, when I told an addiction counselor the difficulty I was having talking to my brothers, she asked me what kind of relationship I wanted with them. I looked at her blankly. She took out a piece of paper, drew seven concentric circles, and used the diagram to explain how we communicate with people on different levels (see Figure 4.1). A paraphrase of her explanation follows.[1]

The area outside the circles represents relationships in our lives that have been cut off, including those clouded by alcoholism. (Family members often believe their only choice is an all-or-nothing relationship.) The rings themselves represent the range of our other relationships—from those in which we sim-

FIGURE 4.1 Concentric Circles Diagram

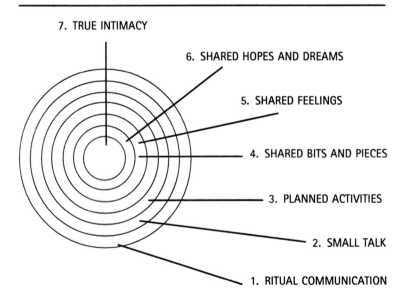

7. TRUE INTIMACY

6. SHARED HOPES AND DREAMS

5. SHARED FEELINGS

4. SHARED BITS AND PIECES

3. PLANNED ACTIVITIES

2. SMALL TALK

1. RITUAL COMMUNICATION

ply acknowledge another person to those in which we enjoy true intimacy.

> *Circle 1:* At the level represented by the outermost circle, we employ "ritual" communication and talk in platitudes: *"Hi, nice to see you, nice weather we're having. How was your vacation?"*

> *Circle 2:* On the next level, we communicate in small talk, or in ways that pass the time. We still don't offer conversation that is very meaningful, nor do we expect it in return. *"Did you see the game last night? How 'bout those Mets?"*

> *Circle 3:* At the third level, we plan activities with the other person. We make a conscious decision to spend time with him. *"Do you want to go for a run at lunchtime tomorrow?"* *"I'm going for coffee. Want to come?"*

> *Circle 4:* On this level, we share bits and pieces of our lives. We tell another person parts of our history and facts about ourselves. *"This is my second marriage."* *"I have high blood pressure."*

> *Circle 5:* At the fifth level, we share our feelings relating to the relationship (both good and bad). *"We have so much in common!"* or *"I feel like I can't do anything right in your eyes."*

> *Circle 6:* On this level, we share our hopes and dreams, our values, and our politics. *"I hope to go to medical school one day if I can afford it"* or *"I'm pro-choice."*

> *Circle 7:* At the center of the circle is the highest level of intimacy, where we withhold nothing. (This is self-explanatory.) There is, of course, one exception: Professionals such as psychiatrists are ethically bound not to share information about a client with anyone. Period.

People move laterally through the circles as they feel emotionally safe. And of course they stay on the outer levels with those who are peripheral to their life, such as the mailman. But if two individuals find they want to move closer, they each must make the choice to do so.

This explanation may sound basic, but it provides a framework for considering the most effective way to communicate with your sibling. It also gives you options. Sometimes a diagram can make things clearer in your mind, or open new pathways. For instance, looking at the circles, you may realize (or decide) that while you'd like a close sibling relationship, you can never attain the most intimate level of communication with your sibling. But there may be another level that is more realistic, and you may decide to fashion a relationship on that level. Or, you may begin to think about moving back and forth among levels. You may even see a reason for staying at the outer levels. Only you know what you feel capable of at any given moment.

You may also realize that your sibling, too, is choosing a level at which he wants to communicate. Being aware of that may help you in deciding whether you want to respond at that level or try for a different one.

A reference book for counselors points out that falling short of finding an effective way to talk to our siblings may only make the situation worse:

> *Effective communication skills are essential in determining our ability to have rewarding relations with others and to achieve satisfaction in life. The quality*

> *of our relationships . . . is dependent on sound com-*
> *munication skills. In fact, it is often our failure to*
> *communicate effectively that leads to personal disap-*
> *pointment and the breakdown of important relation-*
> *ships. Unfortunately, we often leave the success of*
> *important relationships to chance—until communica-*
> *tion fails and the relationships begin to deteriorate.*[2]

Effective communication is important no matter whom you're interacting with, but it can be particularly challenging with an alcoholic brother or sister. Your communication with your alcoholic sibling can be so broken that you're at sixes and sevens when trying to talk to him. And no wonder—it's easy to find yourself at a loss for words when the other person is in denial, or if you're furious at him, or frustrated, and can't find anything nice to say.

When you're at your wits' end with your sibling, it can be especially hard to hear what he's saying. But even if effective communication with your brother or sister is only a dream at the moment, it doesn't hurt, and may just help, to have some hints on how to communicate effectively. You'll find tips at the end of this chapter that, although they pertain to general communication, are especially helpful for talking with your brother or sister.

Other Barriers to Communication

Hopefully you realize it's futile to try to have a conversation with someone under the influence, but communicating with your sibling can be difficult even when he's sober. We mentioned your sibling's possible defense mechanisms in Chapter 3, but there are other obstacles to genuine communication with him as well. First, if you grew up in an alcoholic family, you may have missed out on learning many of the tools for effective communication. Second, if your brother or sister has a co-occurring disorder, it may impose additional burdens. And, third, your sibling probably keeps secrets to hide the things he'd rather you not know.

There are many things I don't know about my brothers. For instance, Ted hasn't had a driver's license in ages. I believe he's paid significant fines and surcharges that accumulated for many years, but I don't know if or when he's supposed to get his license back. It makes sense that Ted, and perhaps your sibling, too, withholds information. They want to maintain their dignity, and I understand that. We've all done things we're not proud of. But it's still disconcerting that there are some important facts I don't know about my brother, and these secrets create a chasm between us.

As Dr. Levounis pointed out, siblings suffering from alcoholism know the pain they cause (although some are surprised to learn the extent). It's one thing for them to tell a therapist or researcher of their misdeeds, and quite another to admit them to family members, especially those who may judge them. But the secrets and lies that are so much a part of the disease are yet another barrier to intimacy. On the other hand, sometimes you know more about your sibling's problems than you care to, such as when others in their lives feel the need to tell you.

Kristen, too, says there is much she doesn't know about Jenna. She knows that, like many people who abuse alcohol and other drugs, Jenna lost her license for a while, but her sister hasn't mentioned whether she got it back or is driving while it's suspended. Kristen also isn't sure of her sister's actual wedding date since Jenna was referring to her spouse as her husband before their actual courthouse ceremony. In addition, Kristen wonders whether Jenna had an unwanted pregnancy once. But the two have never really confided in each other, and she'd be surprised if her sister started to open up now.

The mystery and subterfuge on Jenna's part may sound odd to someone who doesn't have an alcoholic sibling, but to those of us who do—well, we've been there. We're painfully familiar with half-truths, omissions, and the like. Kristen talks as if she takes all the craziness with a grain of salt, but every so often the barrier comes down and she reveals her true feelings. She's confused and concerned and exasperated. She hasn't been able to get close to Jenna, and it hurts. But she's keeping the door open; she saw her sister recently and told her, "Remember I'm there for you if you ever want to talk."

How Others' Lack of Compassion Affects Our Relationship

If you've never heard someone make an unkind comment about your sibling, consider yourself lucky. Several people made such comments to me about my brothers when I was younger and I cringed. If I'd been better at communicating, I would have stood up for myself—and my brothers. At the time, I also bought into the stigma of the disease. Other people's remarks may affect how you, too, communicate with your sibling and how you feel about yourself. Every time someone says something disrespectful about your brother or sister to you, or mentions alcoholism in a disparaging way, it shows a lack of compassion. If you say nothing, you may resent not only the speaker but also your sibling. It may color your perception and hinder communication with him.

I've found the phrase "You are not your family" to be helpful at times like this. It took awhile to sink in when a professional first uttered it, because when people made rude comments about my brothers, it was one thing to know intellectually that I was a separate person but another to internalize it. I needed to be ready with a retort. There's a healthy way to react to comments people make about your sibling, and I now know what I should have said to these ill-mannered folks. A simple statement of fact can be effective. "I don't know why you're telling me this" will get your point across, or perhaps something like "Sorry, but I'm the one here now" or "My sister (or brother) and I are different people." Being ready with a response relates to boundaries, which we'll get into in Chapter 5.

Remember also that part of any shame and embarrassment you might feel if people say something rude is thinking that no one else has experienced what you have. If you hear "You are not your family" (or something similar) often enough, especially from people who have been there and who know you, hopefully you'll begin to internalize it.

Therapy and Your Relationships

We devote an entire chapter to therapy—Chapter 7, on finding support and getting help—but the subject bears mentioning here because of the extent to which it can affect your sibling relationship and other family interactions. In this chapter we introduce attending therapy with your sibling as well other family members (family therapy), whereas Chapter 7 offers a more detailed discussion that includes individual therapy, group therapy, 12-step programs, and the like, for both you and your sibling.

Attending Therapy with Your Sibling

Whether you seek support for yourself or not, one day you may find yourself attending counseling with your sibling as a way to support him. There are several paths that might lead you there. You may approach him about attending, or he may ask you to attend a dual session.

It's understandable if the thought of talking about your sibling's drinking with a professional makes you queasy. You may wonder what's expected of you, and exactly how honest you should be—whether you'll feel safe in saying what you think, whether you'll further alienate each other, and the like. You might also be wondering why you should put forth the effort if he's failed to stay sober for long. These are all valid thoughts that you might bring up with his counselor.

Here are some basic questions you might ask:

- How can you help my sibling and me?
- What will we talk about? In other words, how will this work?
- Whose therapist will you be, technically? Mine or my sibling's?
- How many sessions do you think we'll be having?

- What if one of us decides it isn't working?
- What if other family members want to join us?

Dr. Levounis says:

While this book is designed to help you cope no matter what your sibling's choice (to seek treatment or not), if your brother or sister asks you to attend a therapy session you can play a role in his recovery if you desire. Traditionally, family therapy has focused on the parent-child, husband-wife, or partner-partner relationship when it comes to alcoholism. However, something interesting happens when siblings are included in an alcoholic's treatment. I have found that when a brother or sister attends a *network therapy* session, which we discuss more fully in Chapter 7, the sibling is often the person who moves the therapy forward the most.

In cases where the siblings are close in age, a brother or sister can have a helpful mix of empathy and objectivity. On the one hand, there's an obvious strong bond because they share 50 percent of their genetic makeup (at least in the instance of having the same parents) and typically have grown up together. On the other hand, the siblings often aren't living together by the time they reach therapy and aren't directly linked legally or financially (as parents might be linked to a child, or a husband or wife to a spouse), so they have a certain sense of objectivity. This is not to say that siblings don't have a lot of anger and rage—they're as affected as any family member by alcoholism. But their empathy and objectivity present an inherent advantage when they take part in their brother's or sister's therapy.

During the era when doctors like my father were serving their residencies, the dictum was to treat a patient as you would yourself.

But we found out that this is not a particularly helpful technique. Doctors make terrible patients; we're cavalier, know-it-all, and notoriously nonadherent with treatments—even ones we prescribe for ourselves! Later thinking was that doctors should treat a patient as they would their own child. This was also terrible, because they would often overshoot the target, leading to recommendations that were overzealous. These days we tell residents to think about treating a patient as they would a brother or sister. This seems to be the most helpful way to conceptualize medical care for them—through a combination of empathy and objectivity. These are the same qualities you might bring to your sibling's therapy.

However, if you find your feelings have deteriorated to a point where either your empathy or your objectivity—or both—are missing, then attending therapy with your sibling may not be as effective as it otherwise would be. It may actually be more harmful than beneficial.

Attending Family Therapy Without Your Sibling

If your sibling won't go for treatment, and you and your family are upset about his alcoholism, you might consider attending family therapy as a group, without him. After years of enduring their family being torn apart by her brother's alcoholism, Paula Jones convinced her parents and sister to attend therapy as a unit, and while it got heated at times, she believes most of them benefited from the experience. The family had been focused on her brother for years, which seriously harmed their relationship with one another.

Paula feels Hank is just too toxic to be around. "Family therapy gave both my sister and me the ability to make different choices about being involved with our brother. Also, my parents, my sister, and I learned how to respect the others' choices," she said.

Her father has since passed away and the sisters have altered their relationship with their mother, who is still intertwined with her brother. "We don't spend as much time with her as we used to. I know she feels we have abandoned her to some extent and it makes me very sad sometimes," Paula said. On the other hand, Paula feels as if her mother has chosen her brother over the two women. Still, she's thankful for what family therapy was able to accomplish. The four family members stopped arguing, and all but her mother shifted their focus from her brother.

Paula didn't feel deceptive entering therapy to deal with her brother without him, but you may well feel guilty about talking about your sibling behind his back. You don't have to feel this way. If you've ever flown on an airplane, you've heard the announcement on takeoff that directs parents or caretakers to fasten their own oxygen mask first in an emergency and then to fasten their child's. Attending therapy with your family (or by yourself) if your sibling won't go is based on the same principle. You've got to think of yourself first. If your sibling isn't ready to do anything about his problem, that shouldn't stop you from getting help. You might speak up, however, and say "I've decided to go into therapy about your impact on my life" or "The rest of us are going into therapy as a family because of the impact of alcoholism on our lives."

You may also find, as Paula did, that family therapy changes the family dynamics in ways you're unprepared for. That may be hard to take, but don't lose sight of your initial purpose—to take care of yourself and not allow your alcoholic sibling to overwhelm your life. If another family member doesn't agree with you in therapy, the counselor is there to help work it out.

Severing Ties with Our Siblings— What This Could Mean for You

For their own well-being and that of their children, and for the sake of other family relationships, Paula and her sister would rather not maintain contact with their alcoholic brother. Other siblings would consider this action too drastic. To them, family is family, even with their problems.

Bruce also decided that if his one brother wasn't going to stop drinking (recall that a second brother did stop), he was better off without him in his life. "In the past he made me angry," Bruce said, "but I don't feel that way anymore. Mostly I think that's because he can't hurt me anymore. Now I just feel sad for him, and sorry for the tragic loss of potential. But I don't feel connected in a way that makes me feel compelled to do anything about it."

Rebecca also cut her brother out of her life at one point. When Eddie was out of control and scaring their mother, Rebecca told him she wanted nothing to do with him unless he stopped drinking. But things turned out differently for her than for Paula and Bruce. Now that Eddie has gotten sober, they've repaired their relationship and found a new closeness.

None of these three sober siblings regrets their choice. They feel strongly about family but seem to have been able to detach from their sibling without feeling guilty. This is not to say they banished their brothers from their heart, however, despite Bruce's insistence that he doesn't feel connected to his brother or that his brother can't hurt him anymore. The tie to a sibling is impossible to forget, like it or not, and admit it or not. It may be broken but it can't be eradicated.

When dealing with your alcoholic sibling seems unbearable, you might well lean toward cutting the person off because you don't see an alternative. You may be nearing this point because the relationship with your sibling is harmful to you and your family. However, this decision doesn't make sense for everyone, and cutting your sibling out of your life may affect how you handle other relationships.

In "The Final Cut," an article about severing ties (with anyone) in *Psychology Today,* writer Marina Krakovsky notes it can be difficult to consider that even the most difficult people may have something to offer. However, she writes, "this insight is key to healthy relationships."[3] If a relationship just isn't working—when someone repeatedly violates boundaries—you don't have to put up with it. Krakovsky suggests that a temporary cutoff might be appropriate, but cautions that most experts say a total cutoff should be a last resort. She offers the following strategies if you're leaning toward a full cutoff:

- Ask yourself if there's any benefit to keeping the relationship going.
- See if you can limit contact without ending it entirely, the way ex-spouses might manage a relationship for the sake of their children.
- Don't act in the heat of the moment and don't put down on paper [or write in email] what you might regret later.
- Let bygones be bygones. If you see changes for the better, don't demand a formal apology for past wrongs.[4]

You shouldn't feel guilty no matter what you decide. Every alcoholic is unique, as is every sibling of an alcoholic. You have a responsibility to do what's best for yourself, and what's right for one person may not be right for another.

Dr. Levounis says:

You may well find, at any point in your relationship with your sibling, that without even being prompted he apologizes for past hurts he has inflicted. Step 9 of AA's 12-step program instructs people to make amends for the wrongs they have done. If your brother or sister has been to AA meetings and is working the steps, he may be willing to make amends to you.

You may believe your relationship is past that point. If that's where you are mentally, consider this psychological premise: When we're developing a relationship with someone, a part of us leaves our soul and inhabits the other person. In other words, we give part of ourselves to that person. If that person or our relationship dies, part of ourselves is at large; there's a chunk of our soul floating out there. That's a painful and powerful state of being, especially for a sibling. The process of healing the loss is reclaiming the part of ourselves that is out there. It's a major undertaking. So if at some point you decide to cut ties with your brother or sister, don't underestimate the pain you may end up feeling, because part of yourself has been given to that sibling. The way to make yourself whole again is by reclaiming that part of yourself.

That's the theoretical explanation. In practice, you need to look for alternatives to the part of yourself given to your sibling. Examine the healthy ingredients of your relationship and think about how else you can fill this portion of your life. You may want to resurrect friendships that you have neglected, and re-engage.

Helen, a patient of mine, had several girlfriends and a close re-lationship with her alcoholic brother Harry, but no male friends other than her husband. When she felt she had to sever ties with Harry, she realized he was the only man she knew with whom she was not in a romantic relationship. She missed that relationship tremendously. As part of her healing process she decided to rekin-dle ties with Tony, a good friend from college. They had spent a lot of time together but had lost touch through the years. Through this friendship, she was able to recapture some of the good qualities she had found in her brother.

Let's remember that you're looking to replace the healthy ingre-dients of a relationship with your sibling, not the unhealthy ones. Remember, too, that sometimes the relationship with your sibling can be repaired and restored. One thing that appealed to me about specializing in the treatment of addiction is that frequently, once a person gets sober, a new person emerges—one who is healthy, vi-brant, colorful, and, much to my surprise, more mature and wonder-ful to talk to than I would ever have expected. Because of this dramatic transformation in the person's presentation, I often refer to addiction psychiatry as the surgical aspect of psychiatry. This is not to say he doesn't continue to have the vulnerability to go back to heavy drinking; that's still there, but the alcoholic in recovery has lit-tle reason to despair and much reason to celebrate.

Ensuring Good Communication

Here are some tips on effective communication that may help when talking to your brother or sister.[5]

1. *Listen Effectively.* The first step in developing skilled com-munication is effective listening. Relating to others is

impossible unless you can "fully hear" what they are saying. To begin, try squarely facing and making eye contact with the person with whom you want to communicate. Next, let him or her talk freely while you simply try to comprehend what is being said. Listen for both the feelings and the content of what the person is saying. If you are not sure you have heard everything or understand what is meant, it is often helpful to paraphrase what has been said and then allow the other person to clarify any misunderstanding of the message. Try not to let your own feelings interfere at this point or you might miss something important.

2. *Respond Descriptively.* Be careful not to respond to an important message with an *evaluative* statement. Our culture has programmed us to think largely in evaluative terms—we like something or we don't; we feel things are either "right or wrong." Effective communication is not designed to determine winners or losers. In communicating, the goal is to learn all we can about someone else's thoughts and feelings and to let that person better know the same things about us. This process is quite different from that of negotiation in which individuals may view each other as adversaries. Hence, *descriptive* statements about the other person's communication and your reaction to what is said will be most helpful. *Evaluative* statements are not helpful and tend to elicit defensiveness. For example, you might say, "It sounds like you're having a hard time forgiving Joe." Notice that this allows the other person to elaborate but is not judgmental. You may

then go on to say forgiveness is difficult sometimes, or takes work, and so forth.

3. *Use Your Feelings.* Feelings are important in communicating. Often it takes practice to be able to identify them (and use them constructively), but there is hardly any interpersonal issue about which we do not have some feelings. When you communicate your feelings it is important to be specific and to take responsibility for them. Sometimes this is referred to as an "I" message. For example, "I feel angry because you just left without me, and I really wanted to go along." Note that the statement is descriptive and includes a statement of feelings. It allows the receiver of the communication to respond without feeling accused or threatened. Contrast that with possible reactions to a statement such as "How could you leave me there like that!" or, "You are selfish and inconsiderate," or, "Everyone says you don't care about me." In short, express your feelings, negative or positive, as clearly as possible and be responsible for what you say.

4. *Assess Needs.* Effective communication considers the needs of all involved. If you are giving someone feedback about your reactions to an event, be sure that you are addressing something over which he or she has control. If you do not consider the other person's needs and ability to deal with your communication, your efforts could be destructive.

5. *Make Timely Responses.* Effective communications are delivered at a time when the issue to be discussed is most

important, usually as soon as possible after the behavior which requires discussion has occurred. It can be destructive to save old or unresolved concerns for discussion at a later time or to use them as a weapon ("remember when you . . ."). On the other hand, it is important to decide if the other person is ready to handle your communication immediately. Sometimes, it is best to delay sensitive communications until an appropriate setting can be found for the discussion. Avoid discussing emotional issues until you are in a place where there is privacy and you can talk freely.

In Chapter 5 we'll suggest ways to promote a healthy relationship with your brother or sister—by establishing boundaries. Remember that everyone with an alcoholic sibling feels conflicted; it's an illusion to think otherwise. As my cousin Peter said to me about his alcoholic sibling: "You can love the hell out of your sibling and be mad as hell at him, too."

5

Establishing Boundaries

Maturity involves being honest and true to oneself, making decisions based on a conscious internal process, assuming responsibility for one's decisions, having healthy relationships with others and developing one's own true gifts. It involves thinking about one's environment and deciding what one will and won't accept.

—MARY PIPHER, PSYCHOLOGIST
AND AUTHOR, IN *REVIVING OPHELIA*

T*he word "boundary" can* mean different things to different people. Here's one definition that seems especially appropriate for sober siblings: "the emotional and physical distance you maintain between you and another so that you do not become overly enmeshed and/or dependent." Here's another: "an emotional and physical space between you and another person; a limit or line over which you will not allow anyone to cross."[1]

To say that boundaries are distorted in families in which someone suffers from alcoholism is putting it mildly. My entire family could have served as the model for the type of family Mark Sichel describes in his book *Healing from Family Rifts.* The demarcations between personal rights in my house were, to use his words, "so rigid that they serve[d] as barriers to communication of any kind, or . . . so routinely invaded and overstepped that they create[d] explosiveness, enmity, or ongoing disputes."[2] Our lack of understanding and respecting boundaries dogged my brothers and me for years.

Sichel reminds readers that boundaries are not a rejection of another person; rather, they allow people to live harmoniously with others in mutual respect. In a healthy relationship, boundaries allow us the freedom to disagree, to say no, to make our feelings known when someone insults us, hurts us, or makes us feel uncomfortable, without fearing a backlash. Ideally the other person understands when we speak up, or at least she respects

A boundary is

- The demarcation of where you end and another begins.
- A limit over your physical and emotional well-being which you expect others to respect in their relationship with you.
- The emotional and physical space you need to be the "real you" without pressure from others to be something you're not and without restrictions on how you should think, feel, or act.
- The limits you set on interacting with another so that you can keep your personal identity, uniqueness, and autonomy in the process.

Source: Available online at www.coping.org.

our wishes. By the same token, a person who understands boundaries respects the other person's values and doesn't simply assume things. It sounds so simple, but if we haven't grown up with healthy boundaries, it's not as clear as it seems. We don't always know what appropriate behavior is.

Not only do we have the right to set limits, but we need to do so, for our own welfare. On the other hand, limits that are inflexible can be just as ineffective as having no boundaries at all. We can have so many rules that we close off the possibility of connecting with another person. We may not allow ourselves to forgive and end up painting ourselves into a corner. An alcoholic sibling's transgressions can seem overwhelming, but if we ride that high horse for too long, sometimes it's not easy getting down.

The choices sober siblings make about what we will and will not do are highly personal and vary from person to person. Others cannot tell you what to do if they haven't walked in your shoes. In this chapter we list situations that ask you to consider what your own boundary might be and provide examples of what other people have decided. Dealing with an alcoholic sibling can test even the strongest person when it comes to boundaries, so even if you believe you have set limits and they work well for you, we hope you may still learn something new.

For starters, consider the following list of life events or milestones that are particularly stressful for alcoholics and, hence, may potentially be more stressful for you. By being aware of them, you can be more prepared and ready to set your boundaries.

Crisis Points for Alcoholics

- Holidays
- Moving
- Leaving home for college, the military, first apartment, etc.
- Breaking up with a lover
- Getting married
- Birth (or adoption) of a child
- Getting divorced
- Getting fired
- Returning to work or school after treatment (if not ready to face it)
- Getting promoted
- Changing jobs
- Being charged with DWI (driving while intoxicated) or DUI (driving under the influence)

Some of these occasions or events may find you getting together with your sibling, or getting a call for assistance. Thus, the list serves as prelude to some of the choices posed in the following section.

Boundaries to Consider

Boundaries are important in any association, even in healthy, longtime relationships. When you, your sibling, and other family members know what to expect, there's a better chance that things will run smoothly. Setting limits is not selfish; it can protect your mental and even your physical health.

Dr. Levounis says:

Quite often, when treating a patient, we think in terms of a medical hierarchy. Our first concern is for her physical well-being. We make sure the patient doesn't kill herself. I know it sounds obvious, but if she dies, there's no way we can help her. Our second concern is her therapy. If she doesn't come to treatment, we can't be of any help. Third, we work on improving her life and helping her find joy and happiness.

But even before considering any of the above, we need to think about our own survival as her therapist. Sometimes this is literal, such as making sure we sit close to a door if we're concerned that a patient is dangerous, but at other times it's metaphorical. We have to take care of our own mental well-being as well. This applies not only to the therapist but also to you, the sober sibling—you need to think of yourself first.

As you consider the situations that follow, don't forget to start your decision-making by asking the most fundamental question: What do I need to put in place so as to guarantee my own survival? Often, we jump to addressing our sibling's "core" problem without paying enough attention to the safeguards that are essential for our own continued existence. For example, never take the passenger seat if you suspect that your alcoholic brother is driving under the influence—even if you are trying to get him to a meeting. And don't lend your alcoholic sister money before making sure you have enough to pay your own credit cards.

You might not yet have encountered each of the situations that follow, but one day you may.

Cars and Driving

The media have helped get out the message that you should never let someone drive who's had too much to drink, nor should you ever accept a ride with a driver who's had too much to drink. But the DUI charges constantly being reported in local papers show that we have a long way to go to eradicate drunk driving. In my state alone (New Jersey), according to Mothers Against Drunk Driving (MADD), approximately 30,000 DWI citations are issued every year.[3]

Sometimes boundaries require action, such as taking a person's keys, to protect both yourself and others. If you are in a situation where your sibling (or anyone else, for that matter) has had too much to drink, consider the following tips, which can help you intervene and get the keys so that the person doesn't drive:

1. If it is a close friend, try and use a soft, calm approach at first. Suggest to him that he's had too much to drink and it would be better if someone else drove or if he took a cab.

2. Be calm. Joke about it. Make light of it.

3. Try to make it sound like you are doing him a favor.

4. If it is somebody you don't know well, speak to his friends and have them attempt to persuade him to hand over the keys. Usually he will listen.

5. If it's a good friend, spouse, or significant other, tell him that if he insists on driving, you are not going with him. Suggest that you will call someone else for a ride, take a cab, or walk.

6. Locate the keys while he's preoccupied and take them away. Most likely, he will think he's lost them and be forced to find another mode of transportation.

7. If possible, avoid embarrassing the person or being confrontational.[4]

Bailing Your Sibling Out of Jail

It can be upsetting to think your brother or sister will spend the night in jail. I decided early on that if Ted ever asked me to bail him out of jail for something related to alcohol or other substance abuse, I wasn't going to do it. His addiction had been severe from the start and I wanted nothing to do with the legal ramifications. When Ted did eventually ask me to bail him out, as I knew he would, I refused and he didn't talk to me for years. We needed time before either of us could even broach the subject again.

If you haven't yet been faced with the decision of whether or not to bail your sibling out of jail for DUI, you may be wondering if doing so would be enabling. Whether or not to become involved if your brother or sister is arrested also pertains to boundaries. For example, you may be seen as a "safety net" if your sibling becomes involved in legal problems—someone she can always call in these situations. What *is* your boundary? Do you want to draw the line when it comes to legal problems? It's conceivable that your sibling could be wrongfully arrested, but remember that people suffering from alcoholism are good at manipulating others for their own means (and when they're in recovery, they'll often readily admit this!). She may think it's unfair that she was arrested, but that doesn't necessarily mean she was wrongfully arrested.

Retired Illinois Judge Anthony Montelione, who volunteers in DUI prevention efforts, said that a first-time offense can be powerful motivation for changing one's behavior. It can be the wake-up call your sibling needs. If she's just beginning to show signs of a problem, then the arrest itself may be a warning so that she looks at herself in the mirror and limits the amount she drinks from then on or seeks help for a nascent problem.

But if it's not her first DUI, or if you've felt for some time that this might happen, that's a different story. In such cases, bailing your sibling out, even for a first offense, would allow her to avoid an immediate consequence. And if it's her second or third arrest, it's very likely that bailing her out would actually be enabling.

Phone Calls

No one wants a call from someone who's intoxicated. Bruce, the systems analyst with two brothers suffering from alcoholism, put an end to any future such calls the very first time his brother Nick called him drunk. Bruce told him in no uncertain terms not to do it again and hung up. The words are so simple: "Don't call me when you've been drinking," but you have to be able to say them and not think you're being rude or disloyal. Sometimes we err on the side of being too nice.

What if you're not sure your sibling has been drinking? What if she denies it? Some people hide it well. The *Diagnostic and Statistical Manual of Mental Disorders* (DSM) lists several signs of intoxication, the first two of which you'd be trying to identify over the phone:

- Slurred words
- Memory or attention impairment
- Acting uncoordinated
- Weaving or difficulty when walking
- Rapid or uncontrolled eye movements (called "nystagmus")
- Unconsciousness or coma[5]

Still, there are people who, when intoxicated, are able to stay on topic and avoid slurring their words. If you suspect your sibling has been drinking, there's a good chance it's true. The best action is probably to go with your gut feeling. Regardless of what you can tell for certain, if you are uncomfortable and feel that your boundaries are being pushed, remove yourself from the conversation with a simple "I'll talk with you another time."

What You Will and Will Not Discuss

When people are drinking, they often say things they otherwise wouldn't. If they have never learned boundaries (or are self-centered or immature and don't care), they don't realize there are some subjects other people might find crude or too personal.

There are topics you might discuss with a friend that you might not want to discuss with your sibling, especially if you're not the same sex. If you're not comfortable discussing a certain subject with your sibling—for instance, your marriage or her sex life—or if she says something inappropriate when she's drinking, it pays to speak up. Remember that if you're together, you can just leave.

Here's a sample conversation illustrating what you might say:

> *Your sibling:* I had such a hot night last night.
> *You:* That's a little more information than I need to know.
> Did you hear Mom's buying a new car?

Holidays/Family Get-Togethers

Your family values weigh heavily in your decision about whether to include your sibling on these occasions. If she's simply talkative and giggles too much when she drinks, or if she falls asleep, you may want her there no matter what. But if her worst comes out when she drinks and she ruins the occasion for everyone, it may be wise to tell her she's welcome if she agrees not to drink. This can make your sibling defensive, so you'll want to try not to seem judgmental. You might say something like "I love you and I enjoy being with you when you're not drinking. If you feel you have to drink on the upcoming holiday, then it's best we get together another time."[6]

But what if there's a family function like a wedding? Both Bruce and Kate have been in this position. Neither was happy about their siblings' excessive drinking at a family wedding, but each felt so strongly about family that they decided they'd get through it somehow. Here's Bruce's take on that wedding:

> *I felt very embarrassed, not so much personally, but*
> *for my family as a whole. In my perception, a wedding*

is the first time the two families (those of the bride and groom) meet each other. And there's my brother, totally wasted, getting up in front of everyone at the reception and giving a rambling, maudlin speech that made no sense at all—not to my family, anyway, so how much sense did it make to anyone else? I was somewhat angry, too. But I felt mostly embarrassed for my family collectively.

However, as demonstrated by Paula Jones's decision to exclude her brother from her family celebrations, not everyone is willing to overlook certain behavior just because someone is family. This past year Paula hosted her mother on Christmas Eve and told her she'd have to celebrate with Hank alone the next day because he drank every holiday. As usual, her brother flew into a rage on Christmas Day, so her mother did an "about-face" and left for Paula's house. Hank is still drinking, so Paula plans to continue her new holiday tradition.

Remember that many of us have heightened expectations for the holidays, and that real families rarely live up to idealized images, hopes, and dreams. In families with alcoholism, there are usually extra challenges. It's not just OK to establish boundaries, it's necessary—even at those times when, as during the holidays, the situation is especially difficult and emotionally laden.

Drinking Around Your Sibling

Some families don't serve liquor when an alcoholic family member is at their house. Others drink in front of their alcoholic family members. Still others buy beverages like nonalcoholic sparkling wine and offer those or other nonalcoholic drinks to the alcoholics. Some have decided not to serve alcohol at weddings and on other occasions, or they limit it.

If your sibling is in recovery and aware of her problem, or at least has acknowledged the severity of the situation, *and* if there is an open relationship among family members, you may find the suggestions from the Partnership for a Drug-Free America helpful. This organization proposes that family members have an open discussion and ask the alcoholic questions such as the following:

- Should I keep beer in the basement for company or get rid of it and just serve soft drinks?
- Would you prefer to stay home or go to the party with us?
- Should I avoid having a glass of wine when you're around?
- What should I tell the relatives?
- If your friends show up with alcohol or drugs, should I tell them to get lost or do you want to handle it yourself?

The feeling is that a person in recovery "has a right to participate in decisions, especially those that so directly impact recovery."[7]

Giving/Lending Your Sibling Money

One of the biggest decisions you may face, if you haven't already, is whether or not to give or lend your sibling money. People suffering from alcoholism are often out of work or in a low-paying job. They frequently incur legal and medical bills, must pay for physical damage they've done, are supporting children, and sometimes can't make the rent.

Money is a symbol of several things in our society: success, power, and security, to name just a few. It's also the top source of stress in adults, according to a 2006 study by the American Psychological Association (APA).[8] Money can come between you and your sibling if she asks for a handout or a loan. Or, you may feel you want to help out without being asked.

If you lend money to your sibling, it's wise to draw up a contract and set a payment schedule as you would with anyone. It's a business transaction, and putting the terms in writing is good for everyone involved. That still doesn't ensure you'll see your money again, but it puts your sibling on notice that you don't consider it a gift.

The APA research also found that money is "symbolic of emotional issues that may seem unrelated to your personal finances."[9] If you have ever felt like your sibling's "safety net," that should indicate that your brother's or sister's requests for money bother you. On the other hand, you may be more comfortable financially than your sibling, feel fortunate you didn't get the disease, and want to "make up for it." You may feel you *should* share with your alcoholic sibling. There's no easy or singular answer to this question, and you will have to sort through your own feelings. Bear in mind, however, that if you do give your sibling money, you may be enabling her.

A drug-court counselor I spoke to, who has a sister who suffers from alcoholism, has strict boundaries when it comes to money. She'll help with her sister's son or pets if needed, but she'll never give her money to fix her problems. And she'll never bail her out. What's critical here is checking your own feelings and emotions and determining whether you are enabling.

Letting Your Sibling Stay with You

At some point, your sibling may have no place to stay. Whether or not to allow her to move in with you can present a dilemma. Some family members simply don't want to spend too much time with another sibling; the two are like oil and water. Others don't want to share their physical space with anyone, so if a sibling asks, it's a real problem. Still others would never let an alcoholic sibling share their home, because they fear that her unpredictable behavior may jeopardize family harmony. Yet there are also those brothers and sisters who feel compelled to offer a sibling shelter.

If you do let your sibling move in, it's essential to set ground rules, which are nothing more than boundaries. Vicky Crowley, the policewoman from Ohio mentioned in Chapter 2 whose alcoholic brother Tim suffers from depression, let him move in for a while so he could "get back on his feet," but within weeks he was smoking pot in her house. He denied it, but her husband insisted that he had smelled it and that Tim was lying. Vicki finally asked her brother to leave.

Two boundaries come to mind: When she let Tim move in, Vicki could have given him a date by which he had to find other housing, and she could have said that if she or her husband even suspected he was drinking or taking other drugs while in their house the deal was off. He'd have to leave immediately.

Handling a Situation That Is Dangerous or Unsafe

As much as we don't like to think about it, there may be times when our sibling is a danger to herself and others. It's why we take the keys from her when she's had too much to drink. But there are also other potentially dangerous and even life-threatening situations that require us to take action, and in these cases, the choice is clear. We need to do whatever it takes to ensure everyone's well-being.

Dr. Levounis says:

When your sibling is drunk, safety should be foremost—yours and hers. This is not the time to discuss her drinking. You need to make sure a vase is not thrown your way. As an analogy, we used to think that what a schizophrenic said while hallucinating, for instance, might be significant material for treatment, that it offered a window into the person's psyche. We don't think that anymore. For the most part we ignore the verbal barbs. We have compassion for the patient and are present with her, but our priority is to keep everybody safe.

In similar fashion, when your sibling is drunk she may say loving things about you and your family, or hateful things. Either way, none of these verbal outputs means much. If she becomes violent, our best advice is to go into a safety-first, medical model rather than a psychological *"let me understand what the problem is"* model.

From a safety point of view:

- Get out of the way, and protect any children and elderly or fragile persons who are in the area. Call 911 if necessary.

- Keep knives and guns away from your sibling.

From a medical point of view:

- *Intoxication* can be a medical emergency. If your sibling has had too much to drink, she may experience respiratory distress, which, in turn, may result in coma or death. This is far down the line from slurred speech or the inability to stand. Call 911 if you see signs of respiratory distress, such as fast or labored breathing, or no breathing at all.

- If your sibling passes out, make sure she's on her side so that she doesn't choke on her own vomit (while you're waiting for an ambulance, for example). Again, watch for signs of respiratory distress.

- If she has difficulty standing and falls incessantly, that can be dangerous as well. Try to help her so that she doesn't have an accident. Take her arm and lead her to a couch or bed. Help her into a car, drive her home, and put her to bed—but only after making sure that she is fully conscious and breathing normally. When a person's safety or life is at stake, it's important to take precautions.

- *Alcohol withdrawal* can be a medical emergency as well. Your sibling may have convulsions (also called seizures), which can be dangerous, and withdrawal itself can progress to delirium tremens (DTs), which are serious and can even be lethal. (The DTs are characterized by "severe tremors, confusion, extreme fear, and vivid hallucinations."[10]) Other signs of withdrawal are severe anxiety, sweating, rapid heart rate, tremors, and shaking. Your sibling should be supervised by a professional if she's in alcohol withdrawal. Doctors have wonderful treatments for this condition and know exactly what to do.

- If your sibling enters the hospital or the prison system, it's a good idea to tell the professional staff how much she's been drinking so they can watch for alcohol withdrawal.

Other Events and Situations

We cannot hope, in a single chapter, to cover every situation you could encounter. For instance, you may have to decide whether or not to let your sibling watch your children. Can you take the risk that she'll stay sober, or are you being overly vigilant if you worry? I never felt I could let Ted watch my young son even though he had a young son of his own. When it comes to your children, it's better to be safe than sorry.

Or, if you have more than one alcoholic sibling, do you treat them differently, based on their history? What does your head tell you to do? What does your heart tell you to do? Are they at odds, and if so, which one is best to follow in this particular situation?

You may not feel totally comfortable with your decisions, but if you're struggling with the quandary of what to do at certain times, try asking yourself if you're feeling responsible for your sibling. This question applies to every decision we make when it comes to boundaries and our siblings. Using a "self-assessment" to check on how you're reacting to a situation is a good way to keep yourself sane and safe.

We also haven't discussed the possibility that your sibling might have an extended jail stay for a serious crime, or become incapacitated mentally and require full-time care. These situations go beyond the type of decisions we're talking about. If you have other family members, these are joint decisions that require discussion and planning, preferably with assistance from a healthcare professional.

The concept of time is important in another way when it comes to boundaries. If your brother or sister begins treatment or is in recovery, you may be wondering when you can reasonably let your guard down about the danger of your sibling picking up a drink. There's always a risk of relapse, but experts point to certain time intervals relating to recovery.

Dr. Levounis says:

We have found that there are certain hallmarks of recovery to keep in mind:

- *Three days.* A person who has developed significant physiological tolerance to alcohol experiences the most acute medical withdrawal symptoms within the first three days after she has stopped drinking. She may experience tremors and seizures, and her heart rate and blood pressure may skyrocket. After this period, most of the medical danger—but not all—has passed and she is stabilized.

- *Three months.* During this time, the person is at high risk of relapse. Alcoholics Anonymous often recommends attending "90 meetings in 90 days" in recognition of this early stage, when various brain receptor systems are working hard toward re-equilibrating themselves. (In vivid contrast is the addiction process itself, during which the pleasure/reward centers of the brain are hijacked over the long term.) For the first three months of sobriety, the patient may be going through a protracted withdrawal, which is characterized by lingering physiological sensations that make the person want to drink.

During the drinking years, the receptor systems in the brain had become accustomed to alcohol exposure; now, in sobriety, they have to readjust themselves to life without alcohol. Patients often experience anxiety, insomnia, irritability, restlessness, and general malaise; aggression is sometimes displayed as well.

- *Twelve months.* By this milestone, the person has covered all the holidays, or seasonal markers. Maintenance of sobriety for as long as one year offers significant hope of recovery.
- *Five years.* This more stringent time period is recommended for groups such as impaired professionals. For instance, physicians, dentists, pharmacists, and airline pilots are often required to demonstrate that they've been sober for this long in order to regain their full licenses to practice.

Recovery is work over the long haul for your sibling—and for you, too, if you travel along on her journey. Things do improve with time—from the initial, acute, medically dangerous period, to psychological stabilization, to vocational and social stabilization, and, eventually, to a spiritual one as time goes on. AA says that alcoholism results in a progressive loss of power. A person loses her

- spiritual health.
- professional/vocational health.
- family and interpersonal health.
- mental health.
- physical health.

You can think of recovery as a person regaining these things in the opposite order.

Cutting Off Contact

Severing ties, discussed in Chapter 4, is the ultimate in boundary-setting. As we said, some experts believe this may not be the best way to handle your relationship and may even affect your future relationships with other people. However, you may feel you have to do it, for any of several reasons, such as physical or mental abuse.

We wouldn't begin to tell you what decision is right for you. I, for example, was never able to cut off contact with my brothers completely. I did, however, need breaks following a crisis. Either I waited for them to call me or I called them when I felt able. You may find that approach helpful as well.

Countless other people have wished they had been more understanding of an alcoholic family member. Former presidential candidate George McGovern wrote eloquently about his alcoholic daughter Terry, in the book named for her. She froze to death in a snowbank one night. McGovern said that, looking back, he regrets giving her an ultimatum that he would no longer take her in if she didn't stop drinking. He wished that he had kept on giving her chances in the hope that one day she'd be able to stop.

McGovern's is a moving story. One of the hardest things to do—if not the hardest of all—is to avoid beating ourselves up for the rest of our lives if we give such an ultimatum and the worst happens. The ideal is to not regret our decisions—to not lose ourselves in guilt and recrimination. If we're trying to educate ourselves along with attempting to be supportive, then we're doing the best we can, for ourselves and our families. Even if we give our sibling 100 chances, she may end up in the same place.

Cutting an alcoholic sibling off doesn't mean we're uncaring. What it does mean is that we're doing what is sometimes necessary to prevent our siblings from dragging us down with them. I admit I haven't always been as good at taking my own advice as I would like. One way to set this boundary may be to say that you need to take a break from your sibling for your own sanity, that it's too painful to talk right now and you'll call when you're able.

Dr. Levounis says:

Boundaries are a bit of a paradox. On the one hand, in order to understand another human being's pain you have to be able to blur the boundaries between the two of you and feel what it's like to walk in her shoes, whether you're a therapist or a family member. Inherent in loving someone and in the healing process is the ability to transcend the intersection where "I" end and "you" begin. The trick to sustaining your own sanity and well-being is to allow yourself to sense the other person's fears, hopes, and angst while at the same time being able to step back and re-establish your own boundaries. In this way you can empathize with another person without necessarily having experienced the disease of alcoholism directly. You don't have to suffer from cancer yourself in order to be a wonderful oncologist who can empathize with a person who has cancer.

It is true that shared experience can be a shortcut to establishing rapport. This has been the case with some Greek patients with whom I have a common background. But having similar experiences can also be a detriment to understanding someone. If a patient describes her experience with a Greek church and says, "You know how a Greek church is," it's very tempting for me to say, "Oh, yes, of course I do," even though my experience with Greek churches may be vastly different from hers. In responding this way I may miss an opportunity to really explore what she means.

In psychiatry and psychotherapy, we often talk about a therapist's "blind" spots—areas within the therapeutic interaction where our own fears and insecurities blind us. Indeed, when as therapists we feel personally uncomfortable with certain topics, we may avoid them and unconsciously discourage the patient from exploring these sensitive areas. Equally troublesome are the opposite—what we call "bright" spots, subjects of particular interest to the professional that may overwhelm the relationship. For example, if I myself have experienced alcohol dependence or treatment, it may well become a "bright" spot and affect my ability to treat my patient. This is not to say that therapists who have been addicted themselves are unable to be helpful to someone who suffers from alcoholism. Rather, the point is that such therapists should listen extra-carefully and be vigilant about looking for any undue influence this commonality may have.

Recall from Chapter 2 my discussion of the medical student treating the woman with borderline personality disorder. If the student were more experienced or had been better supervised, she not only might have allowed herself to empathize with the patient's distress about feeling "despicable and ugly" but also might have re-established the boundaries of the relationship and felt good about herself independent of what the patient was attempting to do.

If you feel attacked and the projections coming your way are hurtful, a mental image of wearing a satin graduation gown can be helpful. You're still there, you're present, but you accept the negativity coming toward you into the silky, long garment, and let it slide off. (We do this as therapists when our patients project negative feelings onto us.) Of course, you could also simply end the conversation. But if you decide to stick around while your sibling is projecting her negative feelings onto you, wearing the imaginary gown will not only protect yourself from her insults but also keep your boundaries intact.

Setting boundaries is a way to maintain a relationship with an alcoholic while shielding ourselves from the damage she can inflict. It's regrettable to have to think about protecting ourselves when we're talking about our own sibling. But the disease can make people commit unspeakable acts—acts they would never dream of committing had they not lost their way because of alcohol. If you can master boundary-setting and yet not be rigid, you will help not only yourself but your relationship with your brother or sister as well.

Merely having boundaries will not solve every problem, of course. It can be awfully lonely when someone calls to say that your sibling is in trouble, and when her well-being seems to be riding on you. But your rightful responsibility is to your own family and yourself, which is why it pays to consider what your limits should be.

6

You're Entitled
to Your Feelings

*Each and every family touched by addiction knows the
heartbreak of broken dreams.*

—Vice Admiral Richard H. Carmona,
MD, MPH, FACS, U.S. Surgeon General

Have you ever been so frustrated with your brother or sister
that you could rip metal? As we mentioned earlier, it's not
uncommon to feel a range of strong emotions, such as rage or
disgust, toward your alcoholic sibling. It's also easy to be worried when he's drinking; if he's been in trouble, it can feel like
you're always waiting for the other shoe to fall. At the same
time, you can feel so sorry for him, and so helpless, that it makes
your heart lurch.

Alcoholics may self-medicate to avoid their feelings, but
sober siblings can mask or deny their emotions, too. It's a survival mechanism. This chapter explores some of these feelings,
with a focus on why they occur and what some siblings do in
response to their feelings that they may not even be aware of.

What's Behind Your Feelings

According to experts, when a child has a disability or a serious disease, the family usually circles around, focusing all its energy on him. That may be partly because he requires significant care or because the parents feel guilty, but it can leave the other children feeling left out and angry that one sibling gets center stage.

It may be similar in your family: Your sibling gets most of the attention—because of either his latest crisis or his mood, or perhaps as people try to cover up his drinking or stop him from drinking. Even in adulthood, it's not uncommon to become resentful. Your sibling upsets the balance in your family.

Kristen, whose sister Jenna has battled addiction since her teens, is an example of a sober sibling whose sentiments are caught up in a tug of war. "Confusion, hurt, and anger—those are the main feelings I am feeling," she explained. In our early conversations, Kristen seemed almost detached when talking about her sister, describing their lack of contact matter-of-factly. She admitted resenting Jenna, as if her sister's substance abuse had upset the family apple cart. On the surface, it appeared that Kristen had little affection for her sister. But as I got to know her, she opened up. She was deeply saddened that her sister simply wasn't available to her. This is from an email exchange:

> I am STILL going through things with my sister. She is a mess, she has cut us off completely and it hurts so much. I don't understand why addicts do the things that they do and why they hurt their families. I am angry because she shuts us out, angry because of the

choices she makes and angry because of the constant
lies she tells.

If Kristen truly didn't care about her sister, she wouldn't be so angry. Jenna's problems have grabbed much of the family's attention, but what stand out here are Kristen's despair, ambivalence, and anger. She's having a hard time distinguishing between the person that is her sister and the disease of addiction. When addiction takes such a strong hold and changes a person's behavior so drastically, it can be a challenge to remember there's a difference.

Becoming the "Good Kid"

Some sober siblings take a 180-degree turn from the path their sibling found themselves on. Especially if there's other alcoholism in the family, they may want to distance themselves from the evil they associate with alcohol. As teenagers, they may not want to cause further pain to their parents, so they do well in school, act responsibly, and stay under the radar. Sometimes they overcompensate and become perfectionists or overachievers, becoming known as "the one who never causes any trouble or "the good one." Playing this role may even be a way of getting attention themselves. Several sober siblings I spoke with said they had "become the good kid" on purpose, although some have probably acted subconsciously.

As you've seen throughout and as you know from your own life, having an alcoholic sibling affects your psyche. Your psychological self reacts to the stressor that is your sibling—and your family's response to him. If you believe you have to make up for his bad behavior and be a model of perfection, that belief may limit you. Yet many sober siblings have actually developed some helpful traits as a result of their experiences. We'll discuss these in Chapter 8.

Your Attitude About Alcohol

Several siblings I spoke to reported having strong feelings about alcohol because of their brother's or sister's drinking. Their attitude also affected the amount they drink. Like many siblings, Kristen has shied away from alcohol after seeing how it can mess up people's lives. Rebecca is not averse to drinking socially herself, but she can't abide anyone getting drunk and obnoxious in her presence.

One night, for example, Rebecca was having a drink with a friend in a hotel bar when the two were disturbed by another customer who had obviously had one too many. He was belligerent to everyone in earshot, but he made the mistake of not letting up on Rebecca. She lost her temper and made a scene, telling the man in no uncertain terms what she thought about loud, obnoxious drinkers who impose on others. The bar actually closed early because of the ruckus Rebecca caused on top of the man's behavior.

Dr. Levounis says:

As a sober sibling, you have experienced firsthand the devastation alcoholism can cause and recognize the genetic vulnerability that extends to other family members as well. So when your friends in college tell you, "Come on, let's get plastered. It's Friday night," or if your colleagues say, "Let's go out for a few drinks—it's been a long week," you may be much less inclined to engage in this activity. You know that alcohol has ruined your sibling's life, and you may also recognize that you're at risk because you share a good many genes with him.

Siblings don't have the generational gap to distance themselves. It's one thing to look at alcoholic parents and say, "I'm not going to be like that." But you grew up in the same home as your brother or sister and there are similarities in your environment. It makes sense that you might have strong feelings about alcohol. This attitude may follow you for the rest of your years, so that you drink only moderately, if at all, throughout your life.

At some point you may feel you want to have a conversation with your sibling and tell him your feelings about his illness. Do you sit him down and tell him how frustrated you are? One thing to consider is whether this would be helpful. In the majority of cases, people know what they need to do. If you decide to let your feelings be known, I suggest you couple this with practical advice. Saying "Just don't drink" isn't enough. For instance, if you tell your sibling "I can't take it anymore. I'm so frustrated and worried about you. You need to see the doctor," have a doctor's name and number ready.

Sometimes we assume that our siblings know we care about them, but that may not always be the case. They may need to hear it. So, whether you're angry or not, saying something like "I don't want to see you die" or "I don't want to see our relationship die" is actually meaningful to them.

As for whether voicing your feelings is helpful to *you*, there has been a lot of debate about expressing anger. One argument is that letting your anger out is like lancing a boil. It's cathartic. But the counterargument is that you may end up saying things you didn't intend to say and generate a lot of problems to be rectified in the future.

In the final analysis, it may be best to not respond when someone says something in the heat of the moment. You might even want to rehearse what you wish to say with a counselor or with another sibling.

Forgiveness and Letting Go of Grudges

As we said in Chapter 4, you may choose to keep contact with your alcoholic sibling who's still drinking even though you don't have the kind of relationship you'd like. You may be harboring a boatload of resentment, however, and even if your sibling stops drinking, you may not be able to forget the past. Perhaps you are the type of person who can easily let bygones be bygones, but if you've had these angry feelings for a while, possibly for years, it may take time and patience to mend the relationship.

In Chapter 5 we discussed what you can do to protect yourself, such as establishing boundaries if your sibling won't seek help. This is all well and good, you might say, but it doesn't address all those bad feelings I have. What if I do establish boundaries, but I'm still mad, for instance?

You can choose to hold grudges, or you can find a way to let them go. If you can't eradicate them completely, you can try to minimize the power they have over you. If you don't, you're setting yourself up for physical problems from the stress. We have a right to our feelings, but countless studies have shown that stress and anger are detrimental to our health. We owe it to ourselves to deal with these negative feelings.

Anger, frustration, and sadness are all valid feelings. We're not saying "Just get over them." If it were that easy, there'd be no support groups, and counselors would have far fewer patients. One thing you can do, however, is to allow yourself a set amount of time to *feel* a negative emotion and then move on. Force yourself to think something else, engage in a physical activity to take your mind off things, or pick up the phone and call a friend. Do something to move past the moment.

Another approach is to remember to make your sibling's disease accountable instead of him. As my brother Ted said, paraphrasing from support organizations: "Hate the disease and not the person." You may associate forgiveness with organized religion, but the concept applies outside the religious domain, too. Remember that your sibling might not have committed some of the egregious acts he did if he hadn't been drinking, and if he has an accompanying mental disorder or is co-addicted, that may be even more reason for his bad behavior.

That doesn't mean he's not responsible for his acts; as we've said before, his responsibility is to get treatment. But his denial can keep him from doing that, which is one of the most frustrating aspects of the disease. Making his disease accountable, however, should make it easier for you to find some peace of mind.

To borrow again from *Healing from Family Rifts*, here are a few thoughts that may help you think positively. Sichel offers these as a way of maintaining family connections, but they apply equally well to managing your negative feelings.

- *Don't turn a breach of trust into a resentment.* When family members let you down, or when they perceive that you have let them down, don't let this fester as a resentment. Embrace the idea that human beings are fallible and make mistakes. Turn any contretemps, or disagreement, into an opportunity to find out more about whatever has caused the breach and communicate your certainty that it can be mended.

- *Engage with family members creatively.* Don't fall into ruts of always . . . reacting in the same way. Keep your family members' interests and desires in mind and surprise them every so often with an unexpected gift or by making plans that you know will engage them. Look for different approaches to connection than you may have tried. When you ask a family member "How are you?," give them the sense that you really want to know the answer.

- *Build on your family members' strengths.* Whenever you find a nugget of something upbeat and positive in a family member's attitude, highlight and build on it. Reflect on the good and valuable aspects of your family members and share your happy evaluation with them.

- *When a conflict is minor, keep it to yourself.* As important as it is to communicate with family members when you feel sufficient distress, it's also important to sit on it if the conflict is minor. Learn to keep your negative reactions to yourself until and unless you decide that they're important enough to warrant discussion. If you do talk to the other person, do it in a way that is embracing rather than alienating and destructive.[1]

One of my favorite reminders about letting go and thinking positively is a poem attributed to Ralph Waldo Emerson:

Finish each day and be done with it.
You have done what you could.
Some blunders and absurdities no doubt crept in;
forget them as soon as you can.
Tomorrow is a new day; begin it well and serenely. . . .

Remember That Time Heals

Many people who have suffered loss, trauma, or significant upset have noted the healing power of time. Bruce's sister, in reflecting on her two alcoholic brothers, explains how the passage of time has given her perspective:

> *It was much harder for me to be generous in my feelings with my alcoholic brothers when I was younger. Joe was drunk for about 20 years, and it took quite a few years for me to trust him at all when he stopped. He also had the blessing of coming back into the family to help take care of my father when he was dying. I'd made a few angry comments over the years, and we put some distance between us, but as we age, we are becoming closer. He also married a really nice woman and we were able to go on vacation together. That*

would NEVER have happened except he's attended
AA for 15 years. Finally, I've realized that he is the
keeper of the memories closest to mine in our upbring-
ing . . . we're next to one another in the birth order. I
think the fact that Joe sobered up has really given me
some hope for my other brother Nick but I don't know
how realistic it is, because Joe's really a rare bird.

It may help to know that even therapists have had to cope
with powerful feelings about an alcoholic brother or sister. Connie
Fenton, a family counselor in Delaware, is one of numerous professionals who have gravitated toward a helping profession as a
result of a family member's alcoholism. She's struggled with her
two alcoholic brothers' drinking over the years. "I know I can't
change them, so I work on my response to them," she said. "I try
not to take their problem personally (the *'If they loved me, they*
wouldn't do this' approach). Their problem has nothing to do with
me. They're in the clutches of a powerful, insidious disease."

If and When Your Sibling Recovers

Don't be surprised if your feelings aren't what you expected if
and when your sibling gets sober. Experts describe a "honey-
moon period" after a family member stops drinking, in which
things are going well, you're feeling optimistic, and there's good-
will between you and your brother or sister.[2] This feeling may not
last, however, and your old feelings of distrust may surface. This
is normal. Both you and your sibling, along with other family
members, are adjusting to recovery, and it isn't necessarily easy.

Recall the crisis points for alcoholics that we mentioned in Chapter 5, and be ready for them.

If your sibling does have a relapse, you may experience a terrible letdown. You had so hoped that he would make it. You may feel outrage and hurt—after all, he had stopped! How could he pick up a drink again? Recognize that this is faulty thinking. Don't be too hard on yourself, and try not to revert to old patterns or negative thoughts that aren't helpful. This is not to say you should wear rose-colored glasses—the chance of relapse is high. But as difficult as it is not to dwell on your sibling's recovery, it benefits both of you if you can be supportive while concentrating on your own life. (In Chapter 7, we offer additional thoughts on your role in your sibling's recovery.)

Dr. Levounis says:

When a loved one relapses, not only do you feel let down but your primary feeling is that you've been lied to. Your sibling has promised, *"I'll never do it again."* He has looked you in the eye and said, *"It will be different this time; I'm a different person. I know the beast I'm dealing with now."* So if he relapses, you feel profoundly cheated and betrayed.

When your sibling made these pronouncements, chances are that he was being 100 percent sincere. He absolutely believed it, and he was as honest as you and me when we feel at our purest. One of the biggest problems with addiction is the disconnect between the primary machinery of craving in the most primitive part of the brain, on the one hand, and the frontal lobe, which is responsible for cognition, executive function or decision-making, and communication with the outside world, on the other.

So if you were to ask your brother or sister, "Do you have any cravings for a drink?" you'd be asking the right question, but directing it to the wrong agency. You'd be asking the question of the frontal lobe, which is the only portal for communication we have, but the cravings actually happen at a different site. So even if your sibling does indeed want a drink he can't answer in the affirmative, because he doesn't have full access to that area. And if he's a teenager, the situation is even more confusing: The brain may not even be fully developed, and the hardware for communicating between the frontal lobes and the pleasure/reward areas of the brain is not fully formed.

Think about your sibling's brain as operating with two different forces. One is the rational, thinking brain, which may have every good intention to stay sober. But the other, more primitive force is sometimes stronger, creating havoc in his brain and seeming to have a life of its own. Your best bet is to align yourself with the rational, healthy part of your sibling's brain, in a "you and me against the beast, the primitive, craving part of the brain." In doing so, the two of you are looking at alcoholism in a collaborative way. Should your sibling relapse, think of this as a setback in the war. You and the healthy side of your sibling may have lost a battle, but you haven't lost the war.

Being a sober sibling can be emotionally challenging. It would be so much easier if we could control our feelings or banish the bad ones. But it's important to realize that everyone experiences low points in life, not just alcoholics and their families. It's part of the human condition.

7

Finding Support, Getting Help

Therapy is a great way to distill clarity from the muddy swamp of discomfort. It can turn around how you feel about yourself and your life. It can offer skills for managing the challenges of anxiety or depression. Therapy is a way to find possibilities where you thought none existed, and comfort when ease felt beyond hope.

—MARCIA HILL, PSYCHOLOGIST AND AUTHOR, IN *DIARY OF A COUNTRY THERAPIST*

As we noted in Chapter 6, sober siblings can be in denial, too. Just as your brothers and sisters may avoid seeking help, so may you. Perhaps you tell yourself that things really aren't that bad or that you just don't have time to do anything about what's bothering you, or you find another excuse for not taking action. But eventually you may reach your limit. When you realize you're sad or angry much of the time, or your life feels out of control because you're focusing on your sibling's crises, you may finally admit you can't handle your brother or sister's drinking by yourself anymore.

It's a big step to acknowledge that your life is unmanageable because of your sibling's alcoholism. But to get help is to nurture your own well-being. Going to counseling or therapy (also called psychotherapy) or finding a support group may not change everything, but if you're open to trying one of these options, you may gain insight and find new ways of dealing with things.

In this chapter we take a look at some of the support resources available to you. We discuss the professionals who provide counseling and what to look for in a therapist. We also provide information about resources available for your sibling so that you're aware of her options and can serve as a resource if you like (and if you have the type of relationship that's conducive to your doing so). Remember that your decision regarding what you do for yourself is apart from any decision she makes.

The first half of this chapter covers counseling/therapy, both individual and group, 12-step programs, and other support. In the second half, we discuss these topics as they relate to your sibling, along with detox, treatment programs, and aftercare.

Counseling/Therapy for You

While many people seek therapy today, there are still those who wouldn't dream of seeing a therapist or counselor. Perhaps they mistake therapy for psychoanalysis, made famous by Freud, with its free association, interpretation of dreams, and exploration of repressed anxieties and the unconscious. Or they're embarrassed, or afraid people will talk about them or think they are weak. Attending therapy has a stigma for these people, just as alcoholism has a stigma.

But seeking professional help is a healthy choice for dealing with problems that people are not equipped to handle themselves. "I do not think I'd be alive but for the kind and professional help I have received," writes singer Judy Collins in *The Seven T's: Finding Hope and Healing in the Wake of Tragedy,* published after she lost her son to suicide.[1] And countless others have echoed her thoughts. The singer also discusses her family's alcoholism in this book.

Here's what Paula Jones said about counseling when her brother's alcoholism caused problems for the entire family and they sought help:

> *Therapy can provide some freedom from the impact your brother's or sister's disease has on the family dynamic. You come to understand that people create their own life experiences, and you need to allow that, without allowing someone else's horrible experience to be part of your life experience. Therapy teaches you how to detach from the outcome of your brother or sister's illness, not with anger, but with love. This helps to keep you from falling victim to the disease, too, and with that comes peace for yourself. Your sibling is in the midst of an illness that, if allowed, can not only destroy the alcoholic, but also the people who love her.*

Dr. Levounis says:

The three main types of psychotherapy fall along a continuum. On one end is *supportive psychotherapy,* which focuses on the present and is often used to see a person through a crisis. Supportive therapy is also helpful to patients who have little capacity for self-awareness and poor impulse control. *Cognitive behavioral therapy* (CBT), which falls in the middle, focuses on changing a person's behavior by helping her develop new ways of thinking. The therapist emphasizes an individual's current situation as opposed to what happened in the past. *Psychodynamic psychotherapy,* on the farthest end of the continuum, is more in-depth than the other two. In this case, the therapist goes back to the person's childhood and asks her to open up, with the goal of increasing her self-awareness.

To better understand the difference among these three therapies, consider activities associated with a house. Supportive psychotherapy is akin to straightening up in a house after the dog has run amok. Cognitive behavioral therapy is analogous to remodeling the house somewhat. And psychodynamic psychotherapy is comparable to rebuilding major sections of the house, if not the entire thing. Many therapists use a combination of these psychotherapies.

Individual Therapy for You

Individual therapy can be done by a variety of mental health professionals: psychiatrists, psychologists, social workers, mental health counselors, and psychiatric nurses. Not only do you want to select a counselor with whom you're comfortable, but it's a good idea if the person is also knowledgeable about alcoholism and the family. A psychologist with a Ph.D., for instance, can be extremely helpful, but be aware that some professionals have special training in addiction as well. Titles vary by state. For instance, in New Jersey, the *CAC* designation following someone's name signifies that the person is a certified alcoholism counselor, and in New York State, *CASAC* signifies a certified alcohol and substance abuse counselor. To find the certification or certifications for your state that indicate training in alcoholism and/or substance abuse, try searching the Internet using combinations such as "counselor + alcoholism" or "certification + substance abuse," along with your state name.

Mental Health Professionals: Five Types

Psychiatrist—Has a doctor of medicine (M.D.) or osteopathic (D.O.) degree, with at least four more years of specialized study and training in psychiatry. Psychiatrists are licensed to practice medicine by individual states. "Board-certified" psychiatrists have passed the national examination administered by the American Board of Psychiatry and Neurology. Psychiatrists provide medical and psychiatric evaluations, treat psychiatric disorders, provide psychotherapy, and prescribe and monitor medications.

Psychologist—Has either a master's degree (M.A. or M.S.) in psychology or a doctoral degree (Ph.D., Psy.D., or Ed.D.) in clinical, educational, counseling, or research psychology. Most states license psychologists to practice psychology. They provide psychotherapy as well as psychological testing and evaluations, and they treat emotional and behavioral problems and mental disorders.

Social Worker—Has either a bachelor's degree (B.A., B.S., or B.S.W.), a master's degree (M.A., M.S., M.S.W., or M.S.S.W), or a doctoral degree (D.S.W. or Ph.D.). In most states, social workers take an exam to be

(continues)

Mental Health Professionals: Five Types (continued)

licensed to practice social work (L.C.S.W. or L.I.C.S.W.). The type of license depends on their level of education and practice experience. Social workers assess and treat psychiatric illnesses and provide case management, hospital discharge planning, and psychotherapy.

Licensed Professional Counselor—Has a master's degree (M.A.) in psychology, counseling, or a similar discipline and typically two years of post-graduate experience. Licensed professional counselors may provide services that include diagnosis and counseling (individual, family/group, or both). They have a license issued in their state and may be certified by the National Academy of Certified Clinical Mental Health Counselors.

Psychiatric/Mental Health Nurse—Has either an associate's degree (A.D.N), a bachelor's degree (B.S.N.), a master's degree (M.S.N. or A.P.R.N), or a doctoral degree (D.N.Sc., Ph.D.). Depending on their level of education and licensing, psychiatric nurses provide a broad range of psychiatric and medical services, including the assessment and treatment of psychiatric illnesses, case management, and psychotherapy. In some states, some psychiatric nurses may prescribe and monitor medication.

Source: Adapted from the National Alliance on Mental Illness (www.nami.org).

Note that, although addiction psychiatrists like Dr. Levounis are primarily trained to treat alcoholics and those who abuse other drugs, they treat family members of alcoholics as well.

To find a counselor, you can ask your primary-care physician for a referral or get a name from a trusted friend. Your health insurance provider is another resource. Also, associations such as the National Association of Social Workers (www.socialworkers .org) have online directories.

Here are some questions you might ask the person you're considering. It's perfectly OK to ask. Any therapist who bristles is probably not someone you should go to. In addition, you might feel that you needn't ask all of the questions; for instance, licensing information is available on the Internet, for a fee, on sites such as www.healthgrades.com. You can also check a professional's credentials for free on the website for your state's licensing board. For example, www.medbd.ca.gov is one site for this information in California, and www.armedicalboard.org is a site for Arkansas. Try using search terms such as "doctor + license + board + (state name)."

- Are you appropriately licensed in this state?
- Do you have experience with the situation or condition for which I'm seeking help?
- What is your training? What types of therapy have you been trained in?
- What is your plan for treatment? [Ask this question after your initial interview.]
- What are your expectations of success based on the available research?
- What is the projected length of treatment? [Six months is one suggestion.]
- How will my progress in treatment be measured?
- What treatment alternatives do I have?

You'll also need to check your insurance company's reimbursement policies and look into your mental health coverage.

Once you start therapy:

- If problems arise (e.g., you are not making progress, you're bothered by your therapist's recommendations, you have hurt feelings), make every effort to discuss these issues directly with your therapist, even though this may be difficult.

- If problems persist [and you feel that you aren't receiving the help you anticipated], you may wish to seek a consultation (second opinion) and/or consider new alternatives.[2]

Dr. Levounis says:

"Nancy," a woman who once came to see me, had a brother and a sister who were both alcoholics. Her brother got sober through treatment and hadn't had a drink for ten years. Her sister had also gone for treatment but relapsed, was cited for another DUI, and lost another job. Nancy had a hard time understanding how her brother was able to recover but her sister kept struggling. Her theory was that she'd been able to "get to" her brother but had not succeeded with her sister. She was frustrated because she was closer to her sister than to her brother, and since she hadn't been able to get to her, she felt she had failed.

Our therapeutic focus was on the guilt she felt over what she saw as her sister's lack of success. I tried to convince her that she wasn't responsible for her sibling's success or failure but, rather, was depressed and distraught with worry about her sister. I prescribed an antidepressant and over time her symptoms subsided, though her guilt feelings continued. She continued to talk through her feelings in several sessions and was eventually able to discontinue the medication.

Group Therapy for You

Small groups typically range in size from five to twelve people and are "facilitated" or led by one or two therapists. This approach allows you to bounce ideas off your peers and get their reactions, observe others' social skills (or lack of them), and learn some new ones of your own. As in individual therapy, you might want to discuss events that occurred during the week or specific problems you're having.

Group therapy differs from a 12-step group, in which all members have similar experiences (such as family members who have been affected by alcoholism, or people who overeat). Group therapy members may have some desires that are similar, such as improving their relationships, but the groups are not member-run, as are 12-step groups, nor do they follow a set of twelve principles, such as admitting one can't control an addiction or a way of acting. We describe 12-step groups more fully below. Small-group therapy is usually less expensive than individual therapy.

You might consider individual or small-group therapy at different phases of your life, although some people attend both simultaneously. If you attend individual therapy, your counselor or therapist may recommend small-group therapy for the opportunity it provides to interact with your peers in a facilitated group, or he may recommend a 12-step group.

12-Step Programs/Other Support Groups for You

Support groups, including 12-step groups, are available in a number of places: in your local community, at some religious facilities, at workplaces, and online, for instance. Some hospitals and addiction centers with support groups for alcoholics also have support groups for family members. Therapists can recommend programs and groups as well. Members of 12-step groups are usually paired with a sponsor—a more experienced member—and are usually supported by donations and sales of the group's literature. Below is a sample of some 12-step groups available for sober siblings.

- *Al-Anon* and *Alateen* (www.al-anon.org or www.al-anon
  .alateen.org): Al-Anon, of which Alateen is a part, is perhaps the most widely known self-help group for families of alcoholics. Both groups follow the precepts of Alcoholics Anonymous. Experts suggest that you attend several meetings before deciding whether the group is right for you. If you don't feel comfortable in one group, they suggest you attend meetings in other locations until you find one you feel comfortable with.

- *Families Anonymous* (www.familiesanonymous.org): Families Anonymous is another 12-step program, "a self-help fellowship of families with drug or alcohol users and those with behavioral problems," according to their literature. It is not associated with Al-Anon.

- *Co-Dependents Anonymous* or *C.O.D.A.* (www.codepen dents.org or www.coda.org): A person who is co-dependent focuses on an alcoholic's life rather than on her own. This self-help group offers another option. Its purpose is to help people develop healthy relationships.

Additional Support for You

As Judy Collins says in her book *The Seven T's*, "it's not what happens to us, but our attitude that counts."[3] Some people find their religious beliefs help them deal with alcoholism in their family. Others lean on a network of supportive friends. And don't forget the many things that have been found to help with stress, such as yoga, exercise, journaling, meditation, and acupuncture, for example. The possibilities are endless. Some people believe they can change their thoughts and lift their mood by sheer willpower. It's up to you to find an interest that makes you happy.

If you find that you're feeling extremely upset or vulnerable, and nothing seems to help, your family doctor or therapist can refer you to a psychiatrist, who has even more training than a psychologist and can prescribe medication. This simply means that you're having more difficulty handling (or adjusting to) something going on in your life than one would normally expect or than can be helped by a support group. Sometimes you need the additional help that a psychiatrist can provide.

Counseling/Therapy for Your Sibling

What we said about counseling for you also applies to your brother or sister. For instance, she may be hesitant about attending, and just as it's advisable for you to ask a potential therapist some questions to decide if the person is a good match, so should she. However, the goals of her therapy are very different.

Whereas one of your goals in counseling would be to learn to cope better with your sibling's disease, one goal for your sibling would be to change her behavior regarding drinking—and learn how to avoid a relapse, for instance.

Therapy for your sibling may or may not be part of an overall treatment program for alcoholism, which we discuss in a later section headed "Treatment Programs for Your Sibling." Remember that not everyone with a drinking problem needs an intensive program. There are several options available.

Individual Therapy for Your Sibling

While a counselor might employ cognitive-behavioral therapy when working with your sibling, there are also several other types of therapy used in treating alcoholism. It can be helpful to familiarize yourself with a few of them (such as dialectical behavioral therapy, motivational enhancement therapy, and moderation management) so that you can mention them to your sibling if the subject of therapy comes up, or, if she refers to one, you can say you've read a little about it.

Dr. Levounis says:

Cognitive-behavioral therapy (CBT) is based on principles that are the same for alcoholics as for sober siblings. However, when we employ CBT for alcoholism treatment, we want to change behaviors related to the disease. We go over high-risk, relapse situations with the patient, discuss strategies for avoiding or handling these situations, and help her cope with alcohol cravings. The goal is to change her former habits.

Dialectical behavioral therapy (DBT), commonly used to treat individuals with borderline personality disorder, is now being applied to substance abuse as well. Though based on CBT principles, DBT involves a seesaw type of relationship in which the therapist alternates between support and exploration. When the patient is in crisis, the therapist takes a supportive stand. But when she's in a more stable condition, the therapist can be confrontational and point out some of her maladaptive behaviors. As she becomes more anxious with the confrontation, the therapist then returns to support. This type of therapy involves homework on the patient's part and often phone contact as well.

Motivational enhancement therapy (MET), also known as motivational interviewing, encourages people to rely on their own resources to change their behavior. It's based on Carl Rogers's person-centered approach and the principles of humanistic psychology. MET uses the transtheoretical model of the stages of change. Recall from Chapter 3 that these are precontemplation, contemplation, preparation, action, and maintenance. (Sometimes relapse is considered a stage as well.) The therapist identifies the stage the patient is in and helps her move forward to the next stage. For example, rather than help someone figure out how to stay abstinent for the next year if she has no desire to do that, the therapist might help her simply consider the possibility of change and thus move from the precontemplation to the contemplation stage of change.

Moderation management, as we also explained in Chapter 3, is based on reducing the amount a person drinks. One argument in favor of this therapy is that it's less threatening than committing to complete abstinence, frequently based on a 12-step program. It also allows a therapist to work in the short term with a person who may later enter an abstinence-based program.

Group Therapy for Your Sibling

Your sibling may undergo group therapy on her own or at the suggestion of a therapist, or as part of an inpatient or outpatient treatment program. Group therapy for your sibling is similar to that for you, but the facilitator pays particular attention to a person's alcoholism and other addictions.

Another type of group therapy for your sibling is *network therapy,* developed by Dr. Marc Galanter of New York University, in which the alcoholic and her therapist assemble a supportive group of friends and family to attend therapy sessions with her. The purpose of the group is to serve as a social network to encourage her in recovery.

This is not the same as an intervention, in which friends and family members surprise a loved one with the purpose of breaking through her denial. In network therapy, the alcoholic has agreed to treatment and is working on her recovery.

Dr. Levounis says:

In addition to mutual-help groups (such as Alcoholics Anonymous), there are two major arms in the treatment of the alcoholic: psychotherapy and medication. The professionals in one camp believe that the best approach is a combination of therapy and medication. Those in the other camp say that either one works well by itself. But a few of my colleagues and I have found that medication management—seeing a doctor for medication and having brief counseling sessions—appears to be as effective as formal therapy. Whether further research will fully support this idea is unclear.

I've also found that patients have varying dispositions. Some are attracted to medication but hate "hard chairs" and groups. And others are quite willing to share their experiences in a group but would not ingest anything that comes from the pharmaceutical industry. Insisting that someone has to do both is neither particularly helpful nor fully supported by research. In practical terms, we should listen to the patient's preference and provide the treatment that is most palatable to her and most congruent with her values and lifestyle, and build from there to a more integrated treatment approach for her.

There is some controversy about how useful it is to try to match people with treatment. One study found that everyone who went into treatment (whether it was a 12-step-based program, cognitive-behavioral therapy, or motivational interviewing, for instance) did well, although there was no way to figure out who would do better with what treatment.[4] On the other hand, we're learning that some people do better with therapy while others do better with medication. I believe it's quite helpful to ask the alcoholic about her preference. For patients who attend therapy, probably the most important consideration is that the patient engages with the therapist, provider, or doctor. The greater the patient's involvement, the greater the chances of staying in treatment and, hence, the greater the chances of success.

People who choose to take medications for the treatment of alcoholism can select among three approved by the Food and Drug Administration. The oldest is disulfram, or Antabuse, introduced in the late 1940s. Disulfram blocks a crucial step in the body's ability to process alcohol. A person who drinks alcohol while taking this medication will experience a horrific reaction that includes vomiting and feeling very sick. Yet if a person suffering from alcohol dependence takes it every day and doesn't drink, nothing happens.

Disulfram has not been found to be particularly helpful except for people who are highly motivated or are supervised. Those who might lose their license to practice, for instance, such as doctors or lawyers, are good candidates, although it is also true that people with so much at stake tend to do well with any treatment. People who are extremely obsessive and wake up ravaged by the thought *Should I drink, should I not drink?* are also good candidates. By taking this medication first thing in the morning, they effectively remove the option to drink from their internal debate. On the other hand, disulfram is considered a somewhat outdated form of treating the disease, as it is based on a punitive approach. The field has been moving away from harsh confrontation and punishment to motivation, support, and understanding.

Two newer drugs are naltrexone and acamprosate, both of which decrease cravings for alcohol. They address different cravings, however. A "reward craving" occurs after a person has a drink or two. Then the pleasure-seeking system in the brain goes haywire and the person develops a galloping need to have more alcohol. In the context of the popular AA slogan "One drink is too many, a thousand is not enough," this type of craving reflects the "a thousand is not enough" part.

Naltrexone, or ReVia, blocks the opioid receptor and reduces the hyper-euphoria associated with drinking, thus helping the person to reduce her drinking. For example, if your sibling hasn't had a drink for three months and then goes out and has a beer, she "wakes up" the pleasure-seeking area of the brain—and wants more and more. Before you know it she has relapsed. But if she's been taking naltrexone for the last three months (either in pill form or as a once-a-month injection called Vivitrol) and has a couple of drinks, she'll feel a little high, but not nearly as high as she would without the medication. Granted, she's had a couple of drinks, but this medication gives her more opportunity to think about whether it's worthwhile to continue drinking. With the help of naltrexone, she can give her recovery a chance. She can go back on the wagon and not progress to a full-blown relapse.

The other type of craving is an "abstinence craving," also known as a "relief craving," and it refers to a craving for alcohol to stave off an abstinence syndrome (an outdated term for withdrawal syndrome). The alcoholic has stopped drinking and feels the effect of a protracted withdrawal symptom—anxiety, insomnia, irritability, and general malaise. She craves alcohol in order to feel normal. Patients often report feeling exasperated and sometimes want just one drink in order to go to sleep. But, unfortunately, that one drink leads to another and another and eventually to relapse. In the context of the AA slogan noted earlier, this type of craving reflects the "one drink is too many" part.

The third approved medication, acamprosate, or Campral, is thought to reduce relief cravings and specifically treats the protracted withdrawal symptoms such as irritability, insomnia, and anxiety that serve as triggers to relapse. It increases the chances of continued abstinence since the patient experiences less of a push to have that first drink.

Researchers are also looking at additional drugs. For instance, studies indicate that topiramate, or Topamax, an anticonvulsant that is also used for mood disorders, may reduce cocaine and alcohol cravings. Indeed, we are making strides today that people never thought possible fifty years ago.

Treatment Programs for Your Sibling

An alcoholic may enter a treatment program on her own or because she's been persuaded to. Sometimes it's court-ordered. Often people need more than one program over a period of time because of the high incidence of relapse with alcoholism. While this book is designed to help *you*, at the same time we hope it prepares you to be supportive of your sibling's efforts if she decides to get help. As we said earlier, knowing all you can about alcoholism and treatment options allows you to be an initial resource; however, this doesn't absolve your sibling from learning about treatment or taking responsibility for herself.

Treatment programs are of two types: inpatient (or residential) and outpatient. Here are some of the main differences:

An inpatient program

- may last from a few weeks to more than six months.
- eliminates the need for transportation to and from treatment.
- provides around-the-clock supervision and professional help for managing clients' medical and psychological problems.

- is appropriate for people who live in disruptive environments, have difficult work situations, are at risk for life-threatening withdrawal symptoms, or require care for additional medical or psychiatric conditions.

An outpatient program
- may range from counseling once or twice a week to a single all-day or evening program.
- allows clients to maintain family and social relationships while receiving treatment.
- typically costs less than inpatient treatment.
- may be appropriate for people with adequate social support whose withdrawal symptoms are mild to moderate and who do not have co-occurring medical or psychiatric impairments.[5]

Detox

If your sibling is in alcohol withdrawal, she'll need detoxification, supervised by a professional, in which medication is used to counter the excitatory effects of alcohol on the brain and help avoid the dangerous effects of withdrawal, such as delirium tremens. Detox can be part of either an inpatient or an outpatient program. After undergoing this procedure the first time, a person may believe she no longer has a drinking problem. That is not the case. Detox is often the *first* part of a treatment program, but some people have to experience it more than once before they're realistic about what will help them.

12-Step Programs/Other Support Groups for Your Sibling

Support groups may be part of the treatment program your sibling has entered or may enter. They are offered in many settings, including the community, the workplace, and religious institutions—in many of the places that support groups for family members are offered. They're even found in prisons. Meetings take several forms. In open meetings, for instance, members are free to "tell their story" if they so desire, or to describe how they're working on a 12-step precept. New members are usually assigned a sponsor, who has experience in the program and can aid in the person's recovery.

Here's a sampling of treatment programs for your sibling.

- Alcoholics Anonymous (AA) (www.alcoholics-anonymous
  .org or www.aa.org): Probably the best known of the self-
  help groups for alcoholics, AA believes that a person
  is not able to stop drinking by herself and attempts
  to strengthen her ability to recover. This group offers a
  caring network of peers and a sponsor with experience
  in the program. Thousands of people have been helped
  by AA, but it's not without controversy and is not for
  everyone.

- Women for Sobriety (WFS) (www.womenforsobriety
  .org): This organization is based on the premise that female alcoholics face different issues than men and require a different approach to be successful in their
  recovery.

- Secular Organizations for Sobriety (S.O.S.) (www.cfiwest .org/sos/index.htm): This organization advertises that it's a "non-religious alternative" to 12-step recovery programs.
- Self-Management and Recovery Training (SMART) (https://smartrecovery.org): SMART helps people recover from all types of addictive behaviors.
- LifeRing Secular Recovery (LSR) (www.unhooked.com): According to this organization's approach, the individual strengthens herself rather than surrendering to a Higher Power to recover from an addiction to alcohol or another drug.

Aftercare for Your Sibling

Once your sibling gets sober, an aftercare program can help maintain her sobriety. This might involve continued attendance at 12-step meetings, or whatever else a healthcare provider recommends. Aftercare, like all of recovery, is the alcoholic's responsibility. However, experts suggest that you feel free to ask your sibling about her experiences while recovering as a way to show your support. Here are some possible questions:

- I'd be interested in hearing how your meetings are going, if you feel like talking about them.
- Do you like the other participants? Do you feel you have something in common with them?
- Are you finding that recovery is a struggle for you, or is it going pretty well so far?

- If you feel treatment is not working that well, would you like help in investigating others?
- Are there things we in the family could do to make it easier for you to attend sessions?[6]

Dr. Levounis says:

Sometimes, when a person doesn't do well with therapy and starts saying things such as *I don't like my therapist,* it may be an indication that she needs to stick with it. And that's true not just for your sibling but for you as well. A person who makes a statement like this may be dealing with some tough, anxiety-provoking concerns. In that case, wanting to jump ship rather than face inquiry into the material is most likely a defense mechanism. This is why I said earlier that a person's engagement with a therapist is paramount: When the going gets tough and she stumbles across some particularly painful topics, the strength of the patient-therapist relationship can carry her through.

On the other hand, problems will ensue if the patient-therapist relationship itself isn't healthy. As a way of thinking about this situation, consider the following million-dollar questions I sometimes encounter when treating people who are struggling in couples therapy. They wonder, "Is this just a rough period in our lives, and should we stick with it and hope we come out together on the other side? Or is it a losing war, and should we divorce sooner rather than later?" Theoretically we in the medical community should be able to tell the difference, but in practice it's more difficult to distinguish between a good relationship that's undergoing a rough period, which is not uncommon, and a relationship in which the individuals really don't like each other. Realize that breaking up is always messy. And this applies not only to friendships, romantic connections, business arrangements, and sibling bonds but also to patient-therapist relationships. The idea of separating under the perfect circumstances and at the perfect moment—that is, not before we have given the relationship a fair chance to succeed but also not after it's doomed to failure—is just a fantasy. In retrospect, we almost always end up feeling that we acted either too soon or not soon enough.

This being said, there's a somewhat helpful way out of this conundrum when you have to decide whether to stay with your therapist or move on to work with someone else. The number-one predictor of success for a person's therapy is two-fold: The patient has to like the therapist, and the therapist has to like the patient. It's as basic as that. Trust your instincts on this one. I'm not usually a proponent of the "above all, go with your gut feeling" philosophy, because if people always trusted their instincts, they might end up doing some rather mean things to their fellow humans or, if suffering from alcoholism, go straight back to drinking, for instance. But in this case, I support it. Just as we recommended earlier that you should go with your gut if you think your sibling may have been drinking while you're talking on the phone, the same applies here.

Group psychotherapy has been quite helpful in addiction treatment. One reason is that it offers a peer group whose members not only understand and support the alcoholic but also can call her on her denial. Likewise, peers can recognize early signs of relapse and confront her accordingly. You may have heard of the "dry drunk" state, in which a person isn't drinking but starts exhibiting the behaviors associated with the disease. Indeed, AA often remarks on the "relapse three months before you have your first drink." What experts understand now is that the pleasure/reward pathways in the brain wake up during this time and start exerting pressure on the individual to drink. Even if your sibling has not started drinking again (because she's getting support, for instance), she may begin to exhibit behaviors that put her more and more at risk of relapse.

Perhaps she starts wearing her hair the way she did when she drank, or starts talking about the friends she drank with. The signs may be subtle, but they're clear enough that group members can recognize them as threats to her recovery and say, "Listen, I think you better go to more meetings (or talk to your sponsor, or go back on your medication, or make an appointment to see your doctor)." Group psychotherapy offers some protection against these "dry drunk" states.

Other supports, too, are available to aid in your sibling's recovery. Some of my patients report being helped by herbal or alternative medicine, spiritual healers, prayer, or acupuncture. Just as sober siblings have several means of finding additional support, so do their brothers and sisters.

Earlier in this book Dr. Levounis mentioned the long, hard road that is treatment. He was talking about people suffering from alcoholism, but there are no quick fixes for sober siblings, either. Support *is* available, however, and it can help you come to terms with your sibling's disease, which is the subject of our next chapter.

8

Coming to Terms

According to the medicine teaching, there is no bad person, no crazy person; each person's flaws are part of the wheel of life, which is itself flawless. Each person's struggles are a great mystery to be revealed, each struggle becomes a story, each story becomes teaching, each teaching becomes medicine, and medicine makes the people whole and well in spirit.

—EVAN T. PRITCHARD, AUTHOR, IN *NO WORD FOR TIME: THE WAY OF THE ALGONQUIN PEOPLE*

W*hen they finally get* help, many alcoholics work in recovery organizations helping others like themselves, and I used to fantasize that Ted would eventually do that. I also hoped that Steve would enter his senior years independent and in good health. It's not to be, and so I've had to find a way to live with the way things are.

The First Step—
Understanding Alcoholism

We hope this book has helped you do the same. The first step, as we've suggested, is to educate yourself about addiction so that you're not enabling your brother or sister to continue drinking. Resources on alcoholism abound, from books to TV programs to websites. At the very least, you'll understand more about the disease that has a hold on your sibling. That knowledge, in turn, may also help you get your sibling to treatment if you choose to try.

Kate echoes some of these thoughts when she talks about how she's come to terms with her sister's disease:

> Alcoholism is a no-fault disease. The best we can do is to constantly send the message that we want our siblings to get sober and stay sober; that their drinking affects everyone around them and that there is help. This includes psychotherapy, support groups and rehab, and in some cases, medication.
>
> As their siblings, we are not responsible for their lives. We can love our brothers and sisters and advise them, but in order for them to get the help they need, they need to come to the decision themselves, particularly since they will need to follow through in order to stay sober.
>
> Feeling guilty or worrying all the time is not helpful; these don't get us anywhere. I think taking a stance like the one I've described and sticking to it is a productive way of handling our own need to help, and we may actually reach our sibling at some point this way.

Siblings like Rebecca have seen their brother or sister regain sobriety and a whole new life. Some, like Kate, are crossing their fingers that their newly sober sibling will maintain his or her sobriety. Others, like Kristen, would like to get closer to a brother or sister who seems unable or unwilling to return the feeling. And still others, like Bruce, don't want to try for a better relationship with their alcoholic sibling.

Here's what Kristen, who has been so angry at her sister yet obviously loves her, has to say about finding a resolution she can live with:

> *I've tried everything and my sister is not ready to change or stop, so in the meantime I just have to let her be and let her do her thing. Hopefully one day she'll be ready to stop and to change her life. It is really hard accepting this. I want to help her and I care about her, but it feels like I don't even have a sister and that hurts me very much. I never see her and I rarely ever hear from her. So for now, I just have to focus on my life and accept that she is the way that she is. I just hope and pray that one day she will realize that she is important and that family is important, and that she changes before it is too late.*

Resolving to Take Care of Yourself

Sometimes, finding peace with what you decide might mean reminding yourself that things are tough at the moment but you'll get by. And that's key—to resolve not to let your sibling's addiction get to you, to take care of yourself, and to be realistic. That's not to say you should close the door on hope; just temper it with caution and pragmatism.

Here are some suggestions from Bruce on coming to terms with an alcoholic sibling:

> *Let them go. Their issues aren't about you. You need to take care of yourself and save yourself. That isn't self-ishness, it's an acknowledgment of how things are. In the end, there is nothing you can do to save people who don't want to save themselves. If someone is bent on behaviors that are self-destructive, you can't change that, and it does them no good for you to go down with them emotionally, physically, and financially.*
>
> *Direct your time and energy toward people you can help and who love and need you. Force yourself to do this—it becomes easier the longer you do it. The more you try to save people from themselves, the more it drags the whole process out.*
>
> *Family members who choose to medicate themselves with alcohol are not growing and maturing during that time. If they come out of it, they see the time they spent drinking as wasted time. If they do get sober, for-give them if you can find it in your heart. You can't make them feel any worse than they already do. Don't pile on with your own hurt—you'll regret it later.*

You may find a few people who believe that sober siblings think of themselves as victims. When I mentioned the idea for this book to a recovering alcoholic, for example, she misunderstood my intentions and became defensive. "That's just great," the woman said. "Just what we need—another group that wants to blame us. You people need to work on yourselves." She didn't understand that blaming alcoholic brothers and sisters for their disease was the furthest thing from my mind. But part of what she said is true. Sober siblings do need to do their own work, whatever form that takes. Because you're so closely tied to your sibling, it's not always easy to remain detached and impassive when your brother or sister is drinking. As we said earlier, it can help to acknowledge the effect alcoholism has had on your relationship, explore the issues you're dealing with, and seek support.

Dr. Levounis says:

Recognize two things: First, treatment works. We in the medical community have more options for treating addictions that work alone, or in combination, than ever before, and I have every confidence we'll see more in the near future. Sober siblings don't have to feel alone with a brother's or sister's problem. Take some of the weight off your shoulders and put it on the shoulders of the doctor, the psychotherapist, the social worker, and groups like AA.

Second, however, and just as important is to remember that not all illness is curable. For example, although treatment works for diabetes, there are times when this illness is stronger than currently available treatment and medications. The situation with alcoholism is similar. There will be some people who never agree to get treatment, and also some whose illness is stronger than the treatment and medications currently available.

Family members often think they have only two options: either tough love or enabling. Hopefully this book has given you more options. If you have educated yourself, if you have learned about healthy relationships and how to deal with someone who is not healthy, if you have approached your sibling about treatment, you have done what you could. You've extended yourself for your sibling. There will be people for whom the illness is bigger than anything medical professionals and family members can do. This is true of cancer, it's true of diabetes, and, unfortunately, it's also true of alcoholism. Sometimes you have to incorporate an acceptance of a very difficult condition into your relationship with your sibling, as you might with many other physical and mental illnesses.

Consider this thought-provoking quote from an eccentric TV character talking about family: "Some people believe that before we're born, when we're still in spirit form, we make a deal with the universe. . . . [We] choose the families we're born into. We have different reasons [for doing this], based on the lessons we need to learn."[1]

You may be as hard-pressed as I am to believe that you have an alcoholic sibling because you had some lessons to learn. On the other hand, through adversity we often discover our true measure. It may seem counterintuitive, but contending with your sibling's disease has made you stronger. Like the family members Steven Wolin and Sybil Wolin write about in *The Resilient Self: How Survivors of Troubled Families Rise Above Diversity*, sober siblings are resourceful. You have found "a capacity to bounce back, to withstand hardship and repair [yourself]."[2]

Rebecca seems to have found this to be true:

> *I think now, looking back, that the alcoholism in my*
> *family has been a blessing in a way. It has helped*
> *make me a more intuitive, stronger person. It also*
> *helped me develop my sense of humor, which is grand.*
> *I can see something funny in every heartache, and it*
> *really helps me get through the tough times.*

If the thought of coming to terms with your sibling's disease sounds impossible right now, that's understandable. (I'm better at doing this on some days than others.) We're all on a journey in this life, to see where the road leads us and what's in store. Our relationship with our brothers and sisters is a journey as well— often a tumultuous, rough-and-tumble, head-over-heels excursion that tests our patience and hammers our heart. But we sober siblings also have a third journey, the one to try to make sense of our sibling relationship and to find what works for us.

Looking Beyond Yourself

In Chapter 7 we reminded you of several ways people are good to themselves in the midst of hardship. They turn to their religion, they exercise, or they try acupuncture, for instance. Here's an additional suggestion we'd like to leave you with: Many people who have experienced pain or loss have found that reaching beyond themselves is a way to find happiness. There are thousands of organizations needing volunteers, including the many recovery organizations. When you help others, the rewards come back to you twofold.

In 2006, there were more than 150,000 Al-Anon members in the United States, according to an Al-Anon spokesperson. Thirty percent of those members reported that they have an alcoholic sibling who is still drinking. Fifteen percent of Alateen members reported having an alcoholic sibling.[3] Considering that these figures don't include the siblings in other support groups or in individual therapy, or the substantial proportion who haven't sought support, you get some idea of our numbers.

Sober siblings are part of a vast community whose addicted brothers and sisters have deeply affected our lives. They represent a huge part of the road we've traveled, and the path we've yet to explore. We hope this book has provided some wisdom and solace along the way.

Epilogue

My *brother Ted* died suddenly while I was writing this book. There was no autopsy, so I don't know the cause of death. It could have been any of several things. At his memorial service I learned that he had hepatitis C and also that he was drinking while taking a strong prescription drug to treat it—a dangerous combination. In addition, he had just completed a regimen of chemotherapy after surviving colon cancer. His widow said he was extremely thin at the time of his death, and the medical examiner commented that he appeared to have been very sick. On top of his illnesses, he had fallen a couple of days earlier while drunk and had hit his head. A friend of his thought he might have died from a brain bleed.

It's easier to write about the possible cause of his death than to admit how shocked I was. Yet if I were truthful with myself, I'd have to acknowledge it's surprising he lived as long as he did. Because of his drug use, he was always in danger of contracting hepatitis or AIDS, and as with all alcoholics, his chances of having an accident while drinking were high.

I didn't think I'd be this devastated, but all I can think about is that it's over. He has no more chances to recover, and there's no time to go back and change things between us. In one of our last conversations, I told him that I sometimes wondered if I had challenged him more on his drinking, if years ago I'd found the right words to break through his denial, whether it would have made a difference. He said he wouldn't have listened. Whether he knew it or not, he was letting me off the hook for any guilt I might be feeling.

His widow displayed photos of my brother over the years at his memorial service. The later ones chronicle his descent into illness. I hadn't seen him since visiting after his drug overdose more than two years ago, and the change in his appearance was striking.

The friends who spoke at his service described a man I forgot existed, or one I didn't take the time to see too often. "You were his friend within ten minutes of walking into his house," one said. Then a second buddy said, "John lied. You were his friend within five minutes." One of them revealed that Ted helped support him in his recovery from alcoholism. Imagine that.

My brother got hooked early and faced a monumental battle. Unfortunately, he lost. But to me, he's no statistic. He's the little brother I stirred ice cream with after dinner until it became soup, the gawky kid who joined me in the photo booth on the Asbury Park boardwalk for a twenty-five-cent strip of black-and-white photos. He's the smart, charming guy who, when he was sober, had a kind word and a smile for everyone.

Ted's death was a tragic end to a tragic life. He had such potential. My brother was a talented businessman, but at the end the reality of his last few years butted up against fantasy. His luck had run out, and his failure, professionally, became one more demon to try to face down.

Ted loved his wife and son deeply, even though he couldn't always be present or provide for them. That had to have shamed him terribly. I know he wanted to be a responsible husband and father more than anything. I can still hear the love in his voice every time he talked about his son, and although his wife has a hard time believing it, I know he cherished her.

But my brother was a complex person, and there's no ignoring the side that emerged when he drank. He had huge appetites and a temper to match. For every good tale someone tells about him, there's a humiliating incident, not mentioned, that Ted wasn't proud of. I picture my brother hating himself, silently vowing to do better. When he was released from the hospital after his drug overdose, I told him, "Let's hope you can finally beat this." "I have to have hope," he answered. "It's the only thing keeping me going."

As I mourn my brother, what I can take away from his death that's meaningful is this: I can try to be a little more understanding, a little less harsh, and a little less judgmental when it counts most. And I can reach out more to those I love. As someone said to me recently: Really, when all is said and done, all we have is each other.

Sadly, Ted's widow and I had let his disease destroy our relationship. I admired her immensely, and it was a loss I regretted. We reconciled when he died, agreeing that the rift had continued for much too long. By reaching out my hand to her and Ted's son now, I hope to maintain a tie to my brother and honor his memory.

If I could have that one last conversation with Ted, I'd tell him I realize how sad it is to hold grudges and how important it is to try to forgive. I'd tell him how glad I was that we finally started talking about his disease after too many years of avoiding it. I'd say once more that I wish I could have found more common ground despite his disease. He understood that I had to create distance between us to protect myself, but if I knew then what I know now, I simply would have hugged him more.

I know it's natural to have regrets when a death is unexpected. I simply had no idea how much I'd miss my brother and how much I'd want to do some things over. Ted grew up in a time with fewer resources for treating alcoholism than there are today, when the stigma was even greater, and when family members didn't know as much about the disease as we do now. I'd like to see a day when no one else has to experience losing a family member to alcoholism.

Ted, I hope you're at rest now and have found the peace that so eluded you in life. You were my brother, and I loved you, no matter what.

Acknowledgments

We're indebted to Renée Sedliar, consummate editor and sage, for her vision in helping us shape this book. We so appreciated her sensitivity and suggestions throughout, not to mention her talent. We're also forever grateful to Linda Konner, our agent, who believed in this project and gave so generously of her time and advice. Every first-time author (or any author, for that matter) should be lucky enough to work with both professionals.

We also want to express our gratitude to the following people at Da Capo: Matthew Lore, who lent early support to the book, Cisca Schreefel, and Wendie Carr. To all of you, along with anyone we may have forgotten who helped shepherd the manuscript through, enormous thanks.

A special thanks to Dwayne Mungal, Petros's tireless assistant at The Addiction Institute, who made our lives easier in so many ways while we wrote.

Pat adds

The sun surely shone on me the day Dr. Petros Levounis agreed to be my coauthor. His wisdom and insight added so much to this book, and I'm deeply grateful to him for his contribution. His dedication to this project was truly amazing.

Thanks also to my local writers' group—Amy, Audrey, Caren, Gwen, Janet, Lillian, and Marlene—for being a sounding board and for their unfailing support and kindness during this project. I'm indebted to my friend and fellow writer Irene as well, for reading the draft and lending her medical expertise.

To my husband, Carl, my rock, who stepped in even more than he normally does to allow me the time to write this book, and to my son, Alex, the other light of my life. Thanks, guys. I also am indebted to my brothers, who are in my thoughts every day.

Finally, to all the sober siblings I spoke with, I so appreciate your honesty, your willingness to dig deep, and your generosity in giving freely of yourselves so others may benefit. Thanks for your courage and your time.

Petros adds

Working with Pat Olsen has been nothing less than going on a wonderful adventure with a great friend. Extraordinarily generous, intensely inquisitive, and affectionately patient, Pat has helped me simplify complex psychiatric concepts and give structure to my thoughts. Thanks, Pat.

I am deeply indebted to my teachers, supervisors, and colleagues who have shaped my understanding of the addictive process and the journey to recovery: Drs. Herb Kleber, Ned Nunes, Frances Levin, Phil Muskin, Jack Drescher, Roger MacKinnon, and Ronald Rieder at Columbia University; Drs. Larry Westreich, Sharon Hird, Rob Levy, Annatina Miescher, Jeff Guss, Madeline Naegle, Richard Francis, and Analice Gigliotti at New York University; Drs. Rick Rosenthal, Ronald Lonesome, and Kenn Ashley at St. Luke's and Roosevelt Hospitals; and Drs. John Renner, Mark Kraus, Andrew Kolodny, Judith Martin, and Ed Salsitz at the American Society of Addiction Medicine. Moreover, there are no words to express my gratitude to Dr. Marc Galanter whose scholarship and friendship have been invaluable over the past ten years.

I also would like to thank my fellows, Drs. Steven Lee, Peter Farol, Stephen Ross, Ramon Solhkhah, Lydia Fazzio, Margie Waldbaum-Levinson, Mary Paizis, Liz Cho, and Romulo Aromin, whom I had the privilege of training while director of the Dual Diagnosis Training Unit at Bellevue Hospital in New York. They have given me—and continue to give me— tremendous inspiration.

Special thanks go to Drs. Stephen Ross, Jose Vito, and Bachaar Arnaout, who reviewed in detail the manuscript of this book and offered perceptive suggestions with scholastic precision and clinical insight.

Most of all, I am profoundly grateful to my patients and their families. They have trusted me with some of the most sensitive, tender, and valuable parts of their lives.

Finally, I would like to thank my partner, Lukas Hassel, who has lovingly endured my endless comments both on sober siblings and on everything else.

Appendix A:

About Alcoholism

Below we've provided some basic information about alcoholism, including definitions and signs of trouble.

Alcohol Use and Abuse

For most people who drink, alcohol is a pleasant accompaniment to social activities. Moderate alcohol use—up to two drinks per day for men and one drink per day for women and older people—generally is considered not harmful for most adults. (A standard drink is one 12-ounce bottle of beer or wine cooler, one 5-ounce glass of wine, or 1.5 ounces of 80-proof distilled spirits.) Nonetheless, a substantial number of people have serious trouble with their drinking. The consequences of alcohol misuse are serious—in many cases, life-threatening.

Heavy drinking can increase the risk for certain cancers, especially those of the liver, esophagus, throat, and larynx (voice box). It can also cause liver cirrhosis, immune system problems, brain damage, and harm to the fetus during pregnancy. In addition, drinking increases the risk of death from automobile crashes, recreational accidents, and on-the-job accidents and also increases the likelihood of homicide and suicide. In economic terms, alcohol-use problems cost society millions of dollars per year. In human terms, the costs are incalculable.

What Is Alcoholism or Alcohol Dependence?

Many sources (including the NIAAA, as stated in Chapter 1) define alcoholism, or alcohol dependence, as a disease characterized by four elements: craving, loss of control, physical dependence, and tolerance. However, the American Psychiatric Association, the body that classifies diseases, provides more formal diagnostic criteria for substance dependence (which includes alcohol dependence) in the fourth edition of the *Diagnostic and Statistical Manual of Mental Disorders*. The American Psychiatric Association's definition of "substance dependence" is as follows: A maladaptive pattern of substance use, leading to clinically significant impairment or distress, as manifested by *three (or more) of the following*, occurring at any time in the same 12-month period:

1. Tolerance, as defined by either of the following:
   A. A need for markedly increased amounts of the substance to achieve intoxication or desired effect
   B. Markedly diminished effect with continued use of the same amount of the substance
2. Withdrawal, as manifested by either of the following:
   A. The characteristic withdrawal syndrome for the substance
   B. The same (or a closely related) substance is taken to relieve or avoid withdrawal symptoms
3. The substance is often taken in larger amounts or over a longer period than was intended

4. There is a persistent desire or unsuccessful efforts to cut down or control substance abuse

5. A great deal of time is spent in activities necessary to obtain the substance (e.g., visiting multiple doctors or driving long distances), use the substance (e.g., chain-smoking), or recover from its effects

6. Important social, occupational, or recreational activities are given up or reduced because of substance use

7. The substance use is continued despite knowledge of having a persistent or recurrent physical or psychological problem that is likely to have been caused or exacerbated by the substance (e.g., current cocaine use despite recognition of cocaine-induced depression, or continued drinking despite recognition that an ulcer was made worse by alcohol consumption)

Source: Reprinted with permission from the *Diagnostic and Statistical Manual of Mental Disorders*, Fourth Edition, Text Revision (Copyright © 2000). American Psychiatric Association.

Alcoholism has little to do with what kind of alcohol one drinks, how long one has been drinking, or even exactly how much alcohol one consumes. But it has a great deal to do with a person's uncontrollable need for alcohol. This description of alcoholism helps explain why most alcoholics can't just "use a little willpower" to stop drinking. He or she is frequently in the grip of a powerful craving for alcohol, a need that can feel as strong as the need for food or water. While some people are able to recover without help, the majority of alcoholic individuals need outside assistance to recover from their disease. With support and treatment, many alcoholics are able to stop drinking and rebuild their lives. Many people wonder: Why can some individuals use alcohol without problems while others are utterly unable to control their drinking? Research has demonstrated that for many people, a vulnerability to alcoholism is inherited. Yet it is important to recognize that aspects of a person's environment, such as peer influences and the availability of alcohol, also are significant influences. Both inherited tendencies and environmental influences are called "risk factors." But risk is not destiny. The fact that alcoholism tends to run in families doesn't necessarily mean that a child of an alcoholic parent will develop alcoholism.

Here are some other terms frequently used to describe addiction to alcohol or other drugs. Addiction is:

- chronic—Once an addiction is developed, it will always have to be addressed. An addict may manage to stop using alcohol or other drugs for significant periods of time, but the disease typically does not disappear. Rather, it goes into remission. Should "normal" drug use be attempted, "out of control" use will return rapidly.

- progressive—Addiction gets worse over time. With some drugs, the individual's decline is rapid. With others, such as alcohol, it can be more gradual.

- primary—Addiction is not just a symptom of some underlying psychological problem. Once the use of alcohol or drugs becomes an addiction, the addiction itself needs to be treated as the primary illness.

- terminal—Addiction to alcohol or other drugs often leads to death through damage to major organs of the body. Also, the risks of contracting hepatitis C and HIV rise with use.

What Is Alcohol Abuse?

Alcohol abuse differs from alcoholism in that it does not include an extremely strong craving for alcohol, loss of control, or physical dependence. In addition, alcohol abuse is less likely than alcoholism to include tolerance (the need for increasing amounts of alcohol to get "high"). Alcohol abuse is defined as a pattern of drinking that is accompanied by one or more of the following situations within a 12-month period:

- Failure to fulfill major work, school, or home responsibilities
- Drinking in situations that are physically dangerous, such as while driving a car or operating machinery
- Recurring alcohol-related legal problems, such as being arrested for driving under the influence of alcohol or for physically hurting someone while drunk
- Continued drinking despite having ongoing relationship problems that are caused or worsened by the effects of alcohol

While alcohol abuse is basically different from alcoholism, many effects of alcohol abuse are also experienced by alcoholics.

What Are the Signs of a Problem?

How can you tell whether someone may have a drinking problem? Here are four questions that may be useful in determining the answer. (To help remember these questions, note that the first letter of a key word in each of the four questions spells "**CAGE**.")

- Have you ever felt you should **C**ut down on your drinking?
- Have people **A**nnoyed you by criticizing your drinking?
- Have you ever felt bad or **G**uilty about your drinking?
- Have you ever had a drink first thing in the morning to steady your nerves or to get rid of a hangover (**E**ye opener)?

One "yes" response suggests a possible alcohol problem. And if a person responds "yes" to more than one question, it is highly likely that a problem exists. In either case, it is important that the person see a doctor or other healthcare provider to discuss his responses to these questions. A health professional can help determine whether someone has a drinking problem and, if so, recommend the best course of action.

Even if someone answers "no" to all of the above questions, if he is encountering drinking-related problems with his job, relationships, or health, or with the law, he should still seek professional help. The effects of alcohol abuse can be extremely serious.

The Alcohol Use Disorders Identification Test, or AUDIT, is another tool for determining whether a person's drinking may be a problem (see Table A.1). A minimum score, for nondrinkers, is 0. The maximum score is 40. A score of 8 or more for men (up to age 60) or 4 or more for women, adolescents, and men over 60 indicates that it's highly likely an alcohol problem exists.

TABLE A.1 The Alcohol Use Disorders Identification Test (AUDIT)

Questions	*0*	*1*	*2*	*3*	*4*
1. How often do you have a drink containing alcohol?	Never	Monthly or less	2–4 times a month	2–3 times a week	4 or more times a week
2. How many drinks containing alcohol do you have on a typical day when you are drinking?	1 or 2	3 or 4	5 or 6	7 or 9	10 or more
3. How often do you have five or more drinks on one occasion?	Never	Less than monthly	Monthly	Weekly	Daily or almost daily
4. How often during the last year have you found that you were not able to stop drinking once you had started?	Never	Less than monthly	Monthly	Weekly	Daily or almost daily
5. How often during the last year have you failed to do what was normally expected of you because of drinking?	Never	Less than monthly	Monthly	Weekly	Daily or almost daily
6. How often during the last year have you needed a first drink in the morning to get yourself going after a heavy drinking session?	Never	Less than monthly	Monthly	Weekly	Daily or almost daily
7. How often during the last year have you had a feeling of guilt or remorse after drinking?	Never	Less than monthly	Monthly	Weekly	Daily or almost daily
8. How often during the last year have you been unable to remember what happened the night before because of your drinking?	Never	Less than monthly	Monthly	Weekly	Daily or almost daily
9. Have you or someone else been injured because of your drinking?	No	Yes, but not in the last year			Yes, during the last year
10. Has a relative, friend, doctor, or other health care worker been concerned about your drinking or suggested you cut down?	No	Yes, but not in the last year			Yes, during the last year
TOTAL					

Source: "Helping Patients Who Drink Too Much: A Clinician's Guide 2005," available online at www.niaaa.nih.gov.

Can Alcoholism Be Cured?

Although alcoholism is a treatable disease, a cure is not yet available. This means that even if an alcoholic has been sober for a long while and has regained health, he or she remains susceptible to relapse.

Binge Drinking

Binge drinking is defined as having five or more drinks on the same occasion (i.e., within a few hours). Binge drinking has become a serious problem on college campuses.

Alcohol and Women

Alcohol affects women differently than men. Women become more impaired than men do after drinking the same amount of alcohol, even when differences in body weight are taken into account. This is because women's bodies have less water than men's bodies. Because alcohol mixes with body water, a given amount of alcohol becomes more highly concentrated in a woman's body than in a man's. In other words, it would be like dropping the same amount of alcohol into a much smaller pail of water. That is why the recommended drinking limit for women is lower than for men.

In addition, chronic alcohol abuse takes a heavier physical toll on women than on men. Alcohol dependence and related medical problems, such as brain, heart, and liver damage, progress more rapidly in women than in men.

Alcohol and Older People

Alcohol's effects vary with a person's age. Slower reaction times, problems with hearing and seeing, and a lower tolerance to alcohol's effects put older people at higher risk for falls, car crashes, and other types of injuries that may result from drinking.

Older people also tend to take more medicines than younger people. Mixing alcohol with over-the-counter or prescription medications can be very dangerous, even fatal. Alcohol can make many of the medical conditions common in older people, including high blood pressure and ulcers, more serious. And physical changes associated with aging can make older people feel "high" even after drinking only small amounts of alcohol. So even if there is no medical reason to avoid alcohol, older men and women should limit themselves to one drink per day.

Sources

National Institute on Aging

http://www.nia.nih.gov/HealthInformation/Publications/alcohol.htm

**U.S. Department of Health
and Human Services
Substance Abuse and Mental Health
Services Administration**

http://ncadi.samhsa.gov/govpubs/ph317

National Institute on
Alcohol Abuse and Alcoholism

http://www.niaaa.nih.gov/FAQs/General-English/default.
htm#experience

Department of Labor

http://www.dol.gov/asp/programs/drugs/workingpartners/sab
/addiction.asp

Appendix B:
Resources

Below you will find lists of organizations and books to help and inform alcoholics and their families, followed by a list of alternative treatments for alcoholics.

Organizations
Al-Anon/Alateen Family Groups
1600 Corporate Landing Parkway
Virginia Beach, VA 23454
1-888-4AL-ANON
1-757-563-1600
www.al-anon.alateen.org or www.Al-AnonFamilyGroups.org

National Association for Children of Alcoholics
11426 Rockville Pike, Suite 100
Rockville, MD 20852
301-468-0985
www.nacoa.org

Adult Children of Alcoholics
P.O. Box 3216
Torrance, CA 90510
310-534-1815
www.adultchildren.org

Alcoholics Anonymous (AA)

475 Riverside Dr.

New York, NY 10115

212-870-3400

www.aa.org

The Partnership for a Drug-Free America

405 Lexington Avenue, Suite 1601

New York, NY 10174

212-922-1560

www.drugfree.org

National Council on Alcoholism and
Drug Dependence, Inc. (NCADD)

12 West 21st, 7th Floor

New York, NY 10017

800-NCA-CALL

800-622-2255

www.ncadd.org

National Clearinghouse for
Alcohol and Drug Information

P.O. Box 2345

Rockville, MD 20847-2345

1-800-729-6686

http://ncadi.samhsa.gov

National Institute on Alcohol Abuse and Alcoholism (NIAAA)

5635 Fishers Lane, MSC 9304

Bethesda, MD 20892-9304

301-443-3860

www.niaaa.nih.gov

Substance Abuse and Mental Health Services Administration (SAMHSA)

1 Choke Cherry Road

Rockville, MD 20857

http://samhsa.gov

Join Together

715 Albany Street, 580—3rd Floor

Boston, MA 02118

617-437-1500

www.jointogether.org

Association for Behavioral and Cognitive Therapies

305 Seventh Avenue

16th Floor

New York, NY 10001-6008

212-647-1890

www.abct.org (general)

www.abct.org/members/Directory/Find_A_Therapist.cfm

(to find a cognitive-behavioral therapist)

The Addiction Institute of
New York (Dr. Levounis is director)
1000 Tenth Ave.
New York, NY 10019
212-523-6491
www.AddictionInstituteNY.org

Information and referrals to community services can be obtained from national organizations such as the following:

800-COCAINE

800-ALCOHOL

Narcotics Anonymous (NA)
P.O. Box 9999
Van Nuys, CA 91409
818-780-3951
www.na.org

Girls and Boys Town National Hotline
1-800-448-3000
www.girlsandboystown.org/hotline/index.asp

Books

Beckman, Chris. *Clean: A New Generation in Recovery Speaks Out*. Center City, MN: Hazelden, 2005.

Black, Claudia. *It Will Never Happen to Me: Growing Up with Addiction as Youngsters, Adolescents, Adults*. Center City, MN: Hazelden, 2002.

Dodes, Lance. *The Heart of Addiction: A New Approach to Understanding and Managing Alcoholism and Other Addictive Behaviors*. New York: HarperCollins, 2002.

Fletcher, Anne. *Sober for Good: New Solutions for Drinking Problems—Advice from Those Who Have Succeeded*. New York: Houghton Mifflin, 2001.

Hoffman, John, ed. *Addiction: Why Can't They Just Stop?* Emmaeus, PA: Rodale, 2007.

Mellody, Pia. *Facing Codependence: What It Is, Where It Comes From, How It Sabotages Our Lives*. San Francisco: HarperOne, 2003.

Merrill, Susan. *Accidental Bond: The Power of Sibling Relationships*. Darby, PA: Diane Publishing Company, 1995.

Meyers, Robert, and Brenda Wolfe. *Get Your Loved One Sober: Alternatives to Nagging, Pleading, and Threatening*. Center City, MN: Hazelden, 2004.

Miller, Angelyn. *The Enabler: When Helping Hurts the Ones You Love*. Tucson, AZ: Hats Off Books, 2001.

Moyers, William. *Broken: My Story of Addiction and Redemption*. New York: Viking Adult, 2006.

Volkman, Chris, and Toren Volkman. *From Binge to Blackout: A Mother and Son Struggle with Teen Drinking*. New York: NAL Trade, 2006.

Volpiceli, Joseph, and Maia Szalavitz. *Recovery Options: The Complete Guide—How You and Your Loved Ones Can Understand and Treat Alcohol and Other Drug Problems*. Hoboken, NJ: Wiley, 2000.

Woititz, Janet. *Adult Children of Alcoholics*. Deerfield Beach, FL: HCI, 1990.

Zailckas, Koren. *Smashed: Story of a Drunken Girlhood*. New York: Viking Penguin, 2006.

Alternative Treatments for Alcoholism

Some people have reported success with alternative treatments such as the following, either alone or in conjunction with more traditional treatments. Consult your healthcare provider for more information.

Acupuncture

Alternative Medicine

Herbal Medicine

Hypnotherapy

Meditation

Prayer

Spiritual Healers

Notes

INTRODUCTION

1. From the National Institute on Alcohol Abuse and Alcoholism. Available online at http://www.niaaa.nih.gov/FAQs/General-English /default.htm#groups.

CHAPTER ONE

1. Stephen Bank and Michael D. Kahn, *The Sibling Bond* (New York: Basic Books, 1997), p. xviii.

2. Nick Kelsh and Anna Quindlen, *Siblings* (New York: Penguin Studio, 1998), p. 27.

3. Bank and Kahn, *The Sibling Bond,* p. xv.

4. Jeanne Safer, *The Normal One: Life with a Difficult or Damaged Sibling* (New York: Delta, 2003), p. 39.

5. Ibid., p. 64.

6. Poll conducted by HBO, *USA Today,* and Gallup (2006). Available online at http://www.hbo.com/addiction/understanding_addiction /17_usa_today_poll.html.

7. For example, as Jeffrey Kluger points out in "The New Science of Siblings," "Even siblings who drift apart in their middle years tend to drift back together as they age." (*Time* magazine, July 10, 2006, p. 55).

CHAPTER TWO

1. National Institute on Alcohol Abuse and Alcoholism, Alcohol Alert No. 14 PH 302 (October 1991), *Alcoholism and Co-occurring Disorders.* Available online at http://pubs.niaaa.nih.gov/publications/aa14.htm.

2. Richard J. Francis, ed., *Clinical Textbook of Addictive Disorders,* 3rd ed. (New York: Guilford Press, 2005), p. 251; citing M. A. Walton, F. C. Blow, and B. M. Booth, "A Comparison of Substance Abuse Patients' and Counselors' Perceptions of Relapse Risk: Relationship to Actual Relapse," *Journal of Substance Abuse Treatment,* vol. 19 (2000), pp. 161–169.

3. Statement from Nora Volkow, director of the National Institute on Drug Abuse (NIDA). Available online at http://www.nida.nih .gov/NIDA_Notes/NNV0118N1/DirRepV0118N1.html.

4. Bryce Nelson, "The Addictive Personality: Common Traits Are Found," *New York Times,* January 18, 1983.

5. Conversation with Petros Levounis, May 2007.

6. Ibid.

7. From the Substance Abuse and Mental Health Services Administration. Available online at http://mentalhealth.samhsa.gov/highlights /april2005/alcoholawareness/default.asp.

8. From the National Institute of Mental Health. Available online at http://www.nimh.nih.gov/health/publications/bipolar-disorder /complete-publication.shtml#pub2.

9. Ibid.

10. From the National Institute of Mental Health. Available online at http://www.nimh.nih.gov/health/publications/borderline-personality -disorders.html.

11. Armand M. Nicholi, Jr., ed. *The Harvard Guide to Psychiatry* (Cambridge, MA: Belknap Press, 1999).

12. The information on antisocial personality disorder provided in this chapter has been paraphrased from the following sources: the National Institute of Alcohol Abuse and Alcoholism, *Antisocial Personality Disorder, Alcohol, and Aggression,* available online at http://pubs.niaaa .nih.gov/publications/arh25-1/5-11.htm; http://pubs.niaaa.nih.gov /publications/iss20-1.htm; and http://pubs.niaaa.nih.gov/publications /Social/Module2Etiology&NaturalHistory/Module%202 %20Etiology%20&%20Natural%20History.ppt#286,33,Slide 33.

13. From the National Institute of Mental Health. Available online at http://www.nimh.nih.gov/health/publications/depression /complete-publication.shtml.

14. Statistic cited in Joyce H. Lowinson et al., eds., *Substance Abuse: A Comprehensive Textbook,* 4th ed. (Philadelphia: Lippincott Williams & Wilkins), p. 158.

15. From the Indiana University School of Medicine. Available online at http://www.medicine.indiana.edu/news_releases/archive_01/genetic _alcohol.html.

16. From the Substance Abuse and Mental Health Services Administration. Available online at http://mentalhealth.samhsa.gov/suicidepre vention/risks.asp.

17. From the U.S. Surgeon General. Available online at http://www .surgeongeneral.gov/library/mentalhealth/chapter4/sec2.html.

18. From the National Institute of Mental Health. Available online at http://www.nimh.nih.gov/health/publications/anxiety-disorders /generalized-anxiety-disorder-gad.shtml.

CHAPTER THREE

1. From the journal *Alcoholism: Clinical and Experimental Research* (July 2006), as reported in WebMD at http://www.webmd.com/mental-health/alcohol-abuse/news/20060626/new-clue-on-family-alcoholis-risk.

2. From a discussion on novelty seeking with Petros Levounis, June 2007.

3. From the Department of Labor. Available online at http://www.dol .gov/asp/programs/drugs/workingpartners/sab/addiction.asp#q8.

4. Quoted in Joyce H. Lowinson et al., eds., *Substance Abuse: A Comprehensive Textbook,* 4th ed. (Philadelphia: Lippincott Williams & Wilkins, 2005). p. 594.

5. From the Substance Abuse and Mental Health Services Administration. Available online at http://ncadi.samhsa.gov/govpubs/ph317/.

6. From the Substance Abuse and Mental Health Services Administration. Available online at http://csat.samhsa.gov/faqs.aspx.

7. J. O. Prochaska, C. C. DiClemente, and J. C. Norcross, "In Search of How People Change: Applications to the Addictive Behaviors." *American Psychologist,* vol. 47 (1992), pp. 1102–1114. Available online at www.psychweekly.com/aspx/article/ArticleDetail.aspx?articleid=19.

8. Lowinson, *Substance Abuse,* p. 161.

9. "Helping Patients Who Drink Too Much: A Clinician's Guide 2005." Available online at www.niaaa.nih.gov.

CHAPTER FOUR

1. From a conversation with Vicky Stollsteimer, L.C.S.W., C.A.D.C., Tinton Falls, NJ, July 2007.

2. From *Innovations in Clinical Practice: A Source Book* (Vol. 1, pp. 377–378, "How to Communicate Effectively"), by P. A. Keller and L. G. Ritt (Eds.), 1982, Sarasota, FL: Professional Resource Exchange, Inc./Professional Resource Press. Copyright 1982 by Professional Resource Exchange, Inc. Adapted with Permission.

3. Marina Krakovsky, "The Final Cut," *Psychology Today* (March/April 2006). Available online at http://psychologytoday.com/rss/pto-2006 0323-000009.html.

4. Ibid.

5. Adapted from *Innovations in Clinical Practice: A Source Book* (Vol. 1, pp. 377–378).

CHAPTER FIVE

1. From Coping.org. Available online at www.coping.org/innerhealing /boundary.htm.

2. Mark Sichel, *Healing from Family Rifts: Ten Steps to Finding Peace After Being Cut Off from a Family Member* (New York: McGraw-Hill, 2004), p. 81.

3. From Mothers Against Drunk Driving. Available online at http://www.madd.org/chapter/3400_4190.

4. From the U.S. Department of Transportation's National Highway Traffic Safety Administration (NHTSA). Available online at http://www.nhtsa.dot.gov/people/injury/alcohol/innocent/.

5. American Psychiatric Association, *Diagnostic and Statistical Manual of Mental Disorders,* 4th ed., Text Revision (Washington, DC: American Psychiatric Association), p. 215.

6. From a conversation with licensed marriage and family therapist Katherine Yost, Ph.D., Little Silver, NJ, May 2007.

7. From the Partnership for a Drug-Free America. Available online at http://www.drugfree.org/Intervention/Recovery/Recovery_for_Family_Members#.

8. From the American Psychological Association. Available online at http://apahelpcenter.mediaroom.com/index.php?s=press_releases&item=36.

9. Ibid.

10. Edward V. Nunes, Jeffrey Selzer, Petros Levounis, and Carrie Davies, eds., *Substance Dependence and Co-occurring Psychiatric Disorders* (New York: Civic Research Institute, 2008), p. 15.

CHAPTER SIX

1. Mark Sichel, "Ten Rules for Cultivating and Maintaining Family Connections," in *Healing from Family Rifts* (New York: McGraw-Hill, 2004), pp. 165–167.

2. From the Partnership for a Drug-Free America. Available online at http://www.drugfree.org/Intervention/Recovery/Recovery_for_Family_Members#.

CHAPTER SEVEN

1. Judy Collins, *The Seven T's: Finding Hope and Healing in the Wake of Tragedy* (New York: Penguin Group, 2007), p. 74.

2. From the Association for Behavioral and Cognitive Therapies. Available online at www.abct.org/about.

3. Collins, *The Seven T's,* p. 133.

4. From the National Institute on Alcohol Abuse and Alcoholism. Available online at http://www.niaaa.nih.gov/NewsEvents/NewsReleases/match.htm.

5. Adapted from Center for Substance Abuse Treatment, "Treating Alcohol Problems," *Substance Abuse in Brief,* vol. 3, no. 1 (Winter 2004).

6. From the Partnership for a Drug-Free America. Available online at http://www.drugfree.org/Intervention/Recovery/Recovery_for_Family_Members#.

CHAPTER EIGHT

1. From the episode of *Judging Amy* dated December 14, 1999, as spoken by character Donna Koslowski, court clerk. Available online at http://www.tv.com/judging-amy/presumed-innocent/episode/1761/summary.html.

2. Steven J. Wolin and Sybil Wolin, *The Resilient Self: How Survivors of Troubled Families Rise Above Diversity* (New York: Villard Books, 1993), pp. 5, 6.

3. From e-mail exchanges during May and August 2007 with an Al-Anon spokesperson.

Bibliography

American Psychiatric Association, *Diagnostic and Statistical Manual of Mental Disorders,* 4th ed., Text Revision. Washington, DC: American Psychiatric Association, 2000.

Bank, Stephen P, and Michael D. Kahn. *The Sibling Bond.* New York: Basic Books, 1997.

Collins, Judy. *The Seven T's: Finding Hope and Healing in the Wake of Tragedy.* New York: Penguin Group, 2007

Frances, Richard J. *Clinical Textbook of Addictive Disorders,* 3rd ed. New York: Guilford Press, 2005.

Keller, P. A., and L. G. Ritt, eds., *Innovations in Clinical Practice: A Source Book.* Sarasota, FL: Professional Resource Exchange, 1982.

Kelsh, Nick, and Anna Quindlen. *Siblings.* New York: Penguin Studio, 1998.

Lowinson, Joyce H., et al., eds., *Substance Abuse: A Comprehensive Textbook,* 4th ed. Philadelphia: Lippincott Williams & Wilkins, 2005.

Nicholi, Armand M., Jr., ed. *The Harvard Guide to Psychiatry.* Cambridge, MA: Belknap Press, 1999.

Nunes, Edward V., Jeffrey Selzer, Petros Levounis, and Carrie Davies, eds. *Substance Dependence and Co-occurring Psychiatric Disorders.* New York: Civic Research Institute, 2008.

Safer, Jeanne. *The Normal One: Life with a Difficult or Damaged Sibling.* New York: Delta, 2003.

Sichel, Mark. *Healing from Family Rifts: Ten Steps to Finding Peace After Being Cut Off from a Family Member.* New York: McGraw-Hill, 2004.

Westreich, Laurence M. *Helping the Addict You Love.* New York: Fireside, 2007.

Wolin, Steven J., and Sybil Wolin. *The Resilient Self: How Survivors of Troubled Families Rise Above Diversity.* New York: Villard Books, 1993.

Index

CPSIA information can be obtained at www.ICGtesting.com
Printed in the USA
LVOW11s1118111114

413085LV00003B/6/P